Wives of the Bible

25 Easy Lessons You Can Learn from these
Imperfect Women that Will Radically Transform
Your Marriage

Jolene Engle

DEDICATION

To My Savior, My King and My God,

Apart from you, I can do nothing.

TABLE OF CONTENTS

Introduction   pg. 5
How to Use this Book   pg. 8
The Wife of Influence   pg. 11
The Disrespectful Wife   pg. 24
The Contentious Wife   pg. 28
The Discouraging Wife   pg. 36
The Wife Who Despised Her Husband   pg. 40
The Worldly Wife   pg. 47
The Manipulative Wife   pg. 51
The Wife Who Placed a Higher Priority on Her
Mothering vs. Her Marriage   pg. 57
The Lying and Prideful Wife   pg. 65
The Unfaithful Wife   pg. 69
The Bitter Wife   pg. 74
The Unloved Wife   pg. 83
The Wife Who Cried Out to God   pg. 88
The Redeemed Wife   pg. 95
The Discerning Wife   pg. 99
The Wife of Sweet Perfume   pg. 106
The Wife Who Wasn't a Doormat   pg. 110
The Wife Who Didn't Nag   pg. 117
The Enticing Wife   pg. 121
The Radical Wife   pg. 128
The Respectful Wife   pg. 132
The Submissive Wife   pg. 139
The Wife Who Feared the Lord   pg. 146
The Transformed Wife   pg. 153
The Bride of Christ   pg. 160
Conclusion   pg. 167

Introduction

I love a good story. Stories can cause me to either laugh or cry. Some will challenge or inspire me. And others will bring me comfort, encouragement and hope. Real stories make a big impact on me because I love hearing how someone overcame the odds, faced their fears, or changed themselves for the better. But the greatest stories are the ones that come straight out of the Bible because not only are these stories filled with real people with heartache, pain, anguish and despair, but their stories are written in a Book that is inspired by the Creator of the Universe. There is no better Book that a person can learn from than the Word of God because this Book transforms lives!

> For the word of God is living and powerful, and sharper than any two-edged sword, piercing even to the division of soul and spirit, and of joints and marrow, and is a discerner of the thoughts and intents of the heart. Hebrews 4:12

The reason why I wrote this book for you is because I have a heart for you to grow in the Lord and grow in your marriage. When I was a new Believer, I didn't know how to follow the Lord.

I didn't know how a Godly woman was suppose to act, nor did I know what type of man I should marry, and I didn't even know what a Christian marriage should look like. I was clueless to all things Godly. I had no examples, no role models and no mentors in my life. I was single and alone. But regardless of my past, I was hungry to learn about the Lord and what His Word said to me. However, often times I didn't fully comprehend what I was reading. I didn't know the difference between the Old Testament and the New Testament. I couldn't figure out what a Gospel was and why were there four of them? And where were all the older women that the Bible spoke about who were suppose to teach me how to be a Godly woman? The more I dug into my Bible, the more questions I had.

Now as I look back to that time in my life I fully understand why God did not send me an older woman to help disciple me... it's because God became my Teacher! The Lord led me on a search of every scripture I could find in the Bible that spoke of a wife or woman.

Many times what I learned from this search is that some women chose wise paths while others made foolish decisions. It was through this intense study that I learned how to follow the Lord and conduct myself as a Christian woman. Not too long after I embarked on this study I became engaged and then married my husband, Eric.

Over the past 15 years of my married life I have implemented what I have learned from these women into my own marriage. It is my hope through the writing of this book that what God taught me over 17 years ago, I can teach you. The Word of God radically transformed my life and shaped me into the wife I am today, in spite of my past, and in spite of the hardships I've endured throughout my marriage. With a humble heart and a willing spirit, God will radically transform your marriage, too, if you let Him.

The Lord is the greatest Marriage Counselor because He's all-knowing and because He designed the institution of marriage. He knows you, He knows your husband, and He knows what the two of you need. If there's a problem in your marriage, the Word has an answer for it. My heart is to help guide you in the Truth so you can apply it to your marriage.

Come, take my hand and let's run to our Marriage Counselor, the One who offers us hope and guidance.

In Christ's Love,
Jolene Engle

How to Use This Book

Within these pages you're going to learn about twenty-five different brides, brides that are very much like you and me. You'll read about wives who have been broken, bitter, angry, and proud, while others who were radical, redeemed, discerning, and transformed. Each wife has a story to tell and within each biblical story is a lesson to learn and an application given to apply to your own life. It's through this process of learning, applying and surrendering your life to the Lord that the molding, shaping and transforming of your heart takes place. This process is how your marriage will be radically transformed.

Each chapter in this book is a lesson. In the first part of the book you'll read about wives who didn't make the best choices in their marriages. Following these wives, are wives whose lives were hard; women who endured great heartache and pain. These women will teach us how to respond in our marriage when we're faced with adversity. And the last group of wives are wives who've made wise choices; wives that you and I will want to emulate and pattern our lives after.

I encourage you to read the wives in the order written because I've designed this book to take you on a journey, a journey to transform your marriage, but I must warn you, you're heading into a battle.

This probably isn't what you wanted to hear, is it? But this book will challenge you because it's filled with the Scriptures and the Word of God does not return void.

When you read about these women, you'll have a battle going on within your flesh. It's the same battle I had when I read about these wives and then wrote about them. But this is really a good battle because it's putting our flesh to death.

We bear fruit when we die to our flesh, but Satan doesn't want you to bear fruit and he doesn't want your marriage to get any better, either. When a marriage reflects Jesus Christ, this makes the Enemy angry. So be prepared for the spiritual battle that's about to ensue as you take this journey.

For we are not fighting against flesh and blood enemies, but against evil rulers and authorities of the unseen world, against mighty powers in this dark world, and against evil spirits in the heavenly places. Eph. 6:12 (NLT)

The other area you'll battle with while reading this book is the lies that the Enemy is going to speak into your life. Satan is going to try to condemn you for your past and for the choices you've made throughout your marriage. Be discerning about the Enemy's tactic. Condemnation is never of Jesus Christ. The Lord will never say you're a loser as a wife because it's not in His nature.

There is therefore now no condemnation to those who are in Christ Jesus, who do not walk according to the flesh, but according to the Spirit. Romans 8:1

The difference between being condemned by the Enemy and being convicted by the Holy Spirit is this: Condemnation keeps you from pursuing and growing in Christ while the conviction of the Holy Spirit will draw you closer to Christ and righteous living.

Now on to the wives…

Lesson 1

The Wife of Influence

When I was studying this wife I originally thought I'd title her as, *"The Wife We'd All Love to Slap,"* but I decided to give her a more encouraging title instead; one that's a little more relatable to every wife.

I was a new Believer when I first read about this wife and I've got to tell you, she irked me to no end. I know no one is perfect, but come on now, when was the last time you took counsel from.....

A snake! Really, a snake?

This wife needs no introduction because we all know she's Eve; the wife of Adam, who caused the fall of mankind because she was deceived.

I'm going to spend quite a bit of time on Eve's life, more so than any other wife in this book since so much of her story lays the proper Biblical foundation for us as wives.

Here's her story.....

> And the LORD God commanded the man, saying, "Of every tree of the garden you may freely eat; "but of the tree of the knowledge of good and evil you shall not eat, for in the day that you eat of it you shall surely die." And the LORD God said, "It is not good that man should be alone; I will make him a helper comparable to him." Genesis 2:16-18

> And the LORD God caused a deep sleep to fall on Adam, and he slept; and He took one of his ribs, and closed up the flesh in its place. Then the rib which the LORD God had taken from man He made into a woman, and He brought her to the man. And Adam said: "This is now bone of my bones and flesh of my flesh; she shall be called Woman, because she was taken out of Man." Gen. 2:21-25

Eve was perfect!

She had no baggage.

She had no ex-boyfriends or husbands.

No failures.

No poor decisions and choices.

She had no past. Think about that concept for just a moment?

The girl had a clean slate. She didn't even have parents who jacked her up!

Her mind was pure. Her body was pure. She would have been open and vulnerable, and there wouldn't have been any walls built around her heart.

We can't help but be a little envious of Eve right now, can we? And we certainly can't identify with her either, but give the gal some time!

When Eve's life began, she was created as a *wife*. I think there is such great power in that statement. When I contemplated how this all came down for Eve's life, when God made this choice to make woman, the reality is He could have made Eve anyway He wanted. Yet, He chose to make her a wife. He felt there was an enormous need for this woman to be a man's wife. Wow, the Creator of the Universe knew how much worth a wife would bring to her husband and how important the role of a wife is to God.

Although the world discounts the worth of a Godly wife, the Lord sees otherwise. The first woman He ever created, He created as a wife. As wives, we have a remarkable purpose for the Kingdom of God.

Eve was created as....

- ♥ A helper to her husband.
- ♥ She was comparable to Adam.
- ♥ She was his equal not his less than.
- ♥ God did not create, nor deem women to be second-class citizens. Just because there are many stories in the Bible where men treated their women like property, this does not mean that God agreed with, nor endorsed this behavior.

Then the Master Designer created the institution of marriage.

Therefore a man shall leave his father and mother and be joined to his wife, and they shall become one flesh. And they were both naked, the man and his wife, and were not ashamed. Genesis 2:24-25

Eve's life starts off like a romantic fairy tale; however, her story is Truth. But soon we will see how quickly her actions caused her life to turn into a train-wreck.

Eve Makes 3 Poor Choices.

Poor Choice #1
Eve Questioned God's Word

Now the serpent was more cunning than any beast of the field which the LORD God had made.

> And he said to the woman, "Has God indeed said, 'You shall not eat of every tree of the garden'?" Genesis 3:1

Eve is now contemplating the question of what God said. She's being tempted by the nasty snake to disobey God. Satan has placed seeds of doubt into her mind. *Sound familiar?* We've walked a similar path, haven't we? I don't know about you, but I sure have!

Jesus was tempted by the Enemy too. Let's look to Him as our example and see how He dealt with this problem.

> Now when the tempter came to Him, he said, "If You are the Son of God, command that these stones become bread." But He answered and said, "It is written, 'Man shall not live by bread alone, but by every word that proceeds from the mouth of God.' " Matt. 4:3,4

How did Jesus handle the temptation? He responded by speaking Truth; the Word of God. Have you ever been tempted to disobey God? Do I even need to ask this question? Now are you starting to understand our sister Eve?

As Godly wives, we need to protect our minds from the snares of the Enemy. Satan comes in search of those that he can destroy and devour and he would love to destroy our marriages.

Be sober, be vigilant; because your adversary the devil walks about like a roaring lion, seeking whom he may devour. 1 Peter 5:8

Poor Choice #2
Eve Distorted God's Word

And the woman said to the serpent, "We may eat the fruit of the trees of the garden; "but of the fruit of the tree which is in the midst of the garden, God has said, 'You shall not eat it, nor shall you touch it, lest you die.' " Genesis 3:2-3

Eve makes a grave mistake here. She says, *"Nor shall you touch it,"* but God did not say that. I think it's common practice to distort God's Word especially when we don't know the Bible very well.

Here are some common examples of how we can easily distort the Truth:

We say, *"Cleanliness is next to Godliness."* But this isn't what the Bible says.

The Bible says: *"Let all things be done decently and in order." (I Cor. 14:40)*

For God is not a God of disorder but of peace. (1 Cor. 14:33)

We say, *"Money is the root of all evil."*

But the Bible says: *"For the LOVE of money is a root of all kinds of evil." (1 Tim. 6:10)*

As Godly wives, we need to know God's Word so we're not deceived or tempted to distort the Truth.

Poor Choice #3
Eve Disobeyed God's Word

So when the woman saw that the tree was good for food, that it was pleasant to the eyes, and a tree desirable to make one wise, she took of its fruit and ate. Genesis 3:6

By one wife's choice and actions, she changed the world.

Eve was discontent with the status quo and all that the Lord had given her; therefore, she willingly chose to disobey God. She saw it. She lusted after it. Therefore, she took the fruit and ate it.

As Godly wives, we need to learn to be content with all that the Lord has blessed us with. The more content we become, the less apt we'll be to disobey God. And we all know what happens when one woman disobeys God!

Godliness with contentment is great gain.
1 Tim. 6:6

Eve Was Deceived.

And the LORD God said to the woman, "What is this you have done?" The woman said, "The serpent deceived me, and I ate." Genesis 3:13

Eve was in bad company and she followed the desires of her heart.

As Godly wives, we need to be careful with who we surround ourselves with. Are they people who will influence us or will we influence them? Do they draw us closer to the Lord or away from Him? And are we listening to our hearts or are we listening to the Holy Spirit?

> *"The heart is deceitful above all things, And*
> *desperately wicked; Who can know it?*
> *Jeremiah 17:9*

> *Do not be deceived:*
> *"Evil company corrupts good habits."*
> *1 Cor. 15:33*

Eve Had Influence Over Her Husband.

She also gave to her husband with her, and he ate. Genesis 3:6

And Adam was not deceived, but the woman being deceived, fell into transgression. 1 Tim. 2:14

Hey honey, will you take a bite? Eve was deceived, Adam wasn't. Adam was influenced! There's a big difference between the two. Can you see how we, as wives, have great influence over our husbands?

Think about it. Adam and Eve daily walked with God, *the* Source of Wisdom, yet, Adam still heeded the words of his wife. Adam wasn't hard of hearing. He wasn't busy watching the big game on TV when Eve gave him the fruit. No, Adam knew exactly what he was doing when he ate of it.

> The man said, "The woman you put here with me—she gave me some fruit from the tree, and I ate it." Then the LORD God said to the woman, "What is this you have done?" The woman said, "The serpent deceived me, and I ate." Genesis 3:12,13

Adam, what were you thinking? Why did you eat it? You weren't deceived, you knew better. Perhaps Adam was enticed by his wife's naked body and batting eyelashes? Maybe he wanted to keep the little woman happy? And we all know the saying, *"A happy wife makes a happy life"*. Yep, that woman had her man wrapped around her little finger. Women can lure their men into doing just about anything. Think about what you can get your man to do if you walked around the house naked all day long.

You have great influence over your husband. God may not have given you the position of the head of the home but He sure has given you the position of influencing the one who is. As a wife, you hold a high position of honor. You're a wise counselor, confidant, and an encourager to your husband. Use your influence for godliness rather than for your own personal gain.

Eve Had Broken Fellowship with God

Then the LORD God said, "Behold, the man has become like one of us, to know good and evil. And now, lest he put out his hand and take also of the tree of life, and eat, and live forever"-- therefore the LORD God sent him out of the garden of Eden to till the ground from which he was taken. So He drove out the man; and He placed cherubim at the east of the garden of Eden, and a flaming sword which turned every way, to guard the way to the tree of life. Genesis 3:22-24

Eve lost her home. I like saying it was foreclosed upon! I can certainly relate to Eve because I've lived through that trial. The gal's standard of living went down hill. But that's not the only thing that went down hill. Her relationship with the Lord did as well. Adam and Eve once walked with God in the Garden, but now that time is over, that is, until God's redemptive plan.

So the LORD God said to the serpent...

And I will put enmity between you and the woman, and between your seed and her Seed; He shall bruise your head, and you shall bruise His heel." Genesis 3:15

The Seed spoken here is Jesus Christ; the Messiah. Because of God's redemptive plan, we can now walk with God. The Word became flesh and dwelt among us.

Lessons to Learn from the Life of Eve...

♥ She was *one* with her husband. She was attached to her husband more than anyone else. Every man needs this from his wife. A husband feels admired and honored when a wife shows him this kind of devotion and support.

♥ Eve had no family so it was easy for her to leave and cleave to her husband. This 'leaving and cleaving' Biblical principle is one that you, as a wife, need to be intentional about. You need to make sure you share your heart with your husband more than with anyone else. More than with your mom, girlfriend, sister, etc. This sharing of your heart attaches you to your husband. It softens his heart towards you and it helps him to dwell with you with understanding. Your allegiance and loyalty should be first and foremost to your man more than to any other person, minus the Lord, of course.

♥ Don't be so naive to think you won't be deceived, because we women will be. Getting used to this concept is something I've had to come to grips with. I've had to learn not to be so prideful to think I wouldn't be spiritually deceived. Satan is known as the master deceiver. The reality is, he comes to steal, kill, and destroy and he'd be oh, so happy to take you and me out of the game. Remember, we're in a spiritual battle. Be on guard and allow your husband to protect you. Sometimes our men can understand things better than we can. If you struggle in this area, pray for the Lord to help you get over your pride.

♥ Don't use your influence for your own personal gain.

♥ Don't listen to snakes, ever!

℘ Application ∾

We see in this story just how much influence we have over our husband, so much so, that our men can wander from what is right in the sight of God.

You have tremendous power in the life of your husband, my friend. Use your influence to please the Lord and He'll honor you for it.

As a result of your righteous living, your husband will be drawn to your loyalty, respect, and integrity. Your marriage will grow stronger as a result of all these things.

Through your words and/or actions, attempt to draw your man closer to you and to Jesus Christ. This can be something as simple as making his favorite meal with no strings attached, complimenting him on his leadership in the home, or telling him you'd marry him all over again!

Lesson 2

The Disrespectful Wife

She chose to ignore her husband's request.

She disrespected him in front of his friends and business companions.

Her husband burned with anger over this incident.

A law went out throughout the land because of her disrespectful actions.

So who is this wife?

She's Queen Vashti, the wife of King Xerxes.

Here's her story....

At the same time, Queen Vashti gave a banquet for the women in the royal palace of King Xerxes. On the seventh day of the feast, when King Xerxes was in high spirits because of the wine, he told the seven eunuchs who attended him—Mehuman, Biztha, Harbona, Bigtha, Abagtha, Zethar, and Carcas— to bring Queen Vashti to him with the royal crown on her head. He wanted the nobles and all the other men to gaze on her beauty, for she was a very beautiful woman.   But when they conveyed the king's order to Queen Vashti, she refused to come. This made the king furious, and he burned with anger.   "What must be done to Queen Vashti?" the king demanded. "What penalty does the law provide for a queen who refuses to obey the king's orders, properly sent through his eunuchs?" Memucan answered the king and his nobles, "Queen Vashti has wronged not only the king but also every noble and citizen throughout your empire. Women everywhere will begin to despise their husbands when they learn that Queen Vashti has refused to appear before the king. "So if it pleases the king, we suggest that you issue a written decree, a law of the Persians and Medes that cannot be revoked. It should order that Queen Vashti be forever banished from the presence of King Xerxes, and that the king should choose another queen more worthy than she. Esther 1:9-19 (NLT)

Every wife, at some point in her marriage, has pulled a 'Vashti'! We've chosen to ignore our husbands request to follow them because we don't always want to submit to their headship, and sometimes for good reason.

I can fully understand where Queen Vashti was coming from, after all, the King was drunk and he wanted his trophy wife to be paraded around in front of his buddies so they, as drunkards, could gawk at her. But not every request a husband gives a wife is a request that is senseless or sinful. Many times a husband can just ask for a wife to believe in him or follow his lead, and the wife isn't willing to do so because she's not interested in giving up control.

Or a wife may not want to give up control because of fear. Fear of the unknown. Fear of her husband making the wrong choice. Fear that he'll let her down once again. But that wasn't Vashti's issue. Vashti just didn't want to submit to her husband's dumb antics. I can't really blame the gal, but, regardless of how I feel about the moronic request the King made to her, he wasn't asking her to sin. He simply wanted to act like a proud peacock. He wanted the guys to see how beautiful his wife was because he was proud of her. But instead of showing off his eye-candy wife, Vashti embarrassed *him* because of her blatant disrespect by refusing to listen to his request.

Vashti got banished from the King's land but that's not something that will likely happen to you or me if and when we choose to be disrespectful towards our husbands. However, we do run the risk of being cast out from the land of our man's *heart*. A husband is designed to need his wife's respect, just like a wife is designed to need her husband's love.

Lessons to Learn from the Life of Vashti...

- ♥ Following her husband's leadership would have saved her a lot of grief.

- ♥ Vashti's sense of pride kept her from respecting her husband.

❧ Application ❧

Give your man respect even if he does something that you deem to be senseless. Your willingness to respect your husband in spite of his flaws and his antics will bring honor to your Lord and your husband.

As hard as it might be for you, don't let your pride keep you from following your man's leadership. Submit to him, but not his sin.

Lesson 3

The Contentious Wife

I so get this woman.

Controlling.

Jealous.

Discontent.

Most wives can identify with her, unless of course you're a dead wife!

So who is this wife?

She's Sarai, the wife of Abraham.

There's so much we can learn from Sarai, however, you might know her as Sarah, but in this lesson, she's Sarai.

I'll introduce Sarah to you later in the book. But before I share her story, first, let me give you the definition of contentious:

1. Given to contention; quarrelsome.
2. Involving or likely to cause contention; controversial
3. Tending to argue or quarrel
4. Causing or characterized by dispute

I laughed at this list because I totally get it! We contend with our husbands when we want to be in charge or in control. Some women can be very vocal about wanting to be in charge, while others can be ever so quiet, yet totally manipulative.

Now let me give you the reason why we become contentious. Remember Eve who ate the forbidden fruit? We'll she got busted and God had to chastise her for her disobedience.

Here was her consequence:

> Then he said to the woman, "I will sharpen the pain of your pregnancy, and in pain you will give birth. And you will desire to control your husband, but he will rule over you. Genesis 3:16 (NLT)

Due to the Fall of mankind, sin entered into our hearts, more specifically, wives all around the world will have the sin-nature of wanting to control their husband.

God deemed it best to establish the husband as the head of the home. The sooner we surrender to God's plan for His design of marriage, the better our marriage will become.

> But I want you to know that the head of every man is Christ, the head of woman is man, and the head of Christ is God. 1 Corinthians 11:3

By surrendering our will to the Lord in our marriage, this act of devotion and obedience to the Lord will point others to Jesus Christ.

Okay, so now do you feel better in knowing that there's nothing wrong with you when you argue, fuss and fight with your man? There's nothing wrong with your man, either. It's just a part of our sinful nature to want to control our Knight in Shining Armor. However, we have the Power to overcome this tendency.

Now on to Sarai's story...

> Now Sarai, Abram's wife, had borne him no children. But she had an Egyptian maidservant named Hagar; so she said to Abram, "The LORD has kept me from having children. Go, sleep with my maidservant; perhaps I can build a family through her." Abram agreed to what Sarai said. So after Abram had been living in Canaan ten years, Sarai his wife took her Egyptian maidservant Hagar and gave her to her husband to be his wife.

He slept with Hagar, and she conceived. When she knew she was pregnant, she began to despise her mistress. Then Sarai said to Abram, "You are responsible for the wrong I am suffering. I put my servant in your arms, and now that she knows she is pregnant, she despises me. May the LORD judge between you and me." "Your servant is in your hands," Abram said. "Do with her whatever you think best." Then Sarai mistreated Hagar; so she fled from her. Genesis 16:1-6

The theme of Sarai and Abram's story is the promise to make Abram a father of many nations. So the couple, in their old age waited and waited for that promise to be fulfilled. But Sarai became desperate. She *really* wanted to have a baby, so she took matters into her own hands. She told her husband to go have sex with another woman. Oh, yes she did! Imagine that? I doubt that he objected to that request from his wife. In fact, she probably didn't have to nag him about it either! "*Sleep with my maid,*" she said.

Think about her for just a second. She's been promised by God that her husband would be the father of many nations. They leave their home to follow God's leading, yet still no baby. Infertility back then was viewed as a woman being in sin and Sarai was humiliated because of her barrenness. So what does a woman do after waiting 10 yrs. for a child that was promised by God? She helps God deliver on His promise, of course! Yep, that's what we wives do.

We think if things are not happening according to *our* plan, of course God needs us to intervene because He may not know what He's doing. (Note my sarcasm here.)

So Sarai figures out a way to fix her problem. *"Oh, husband of mine, can you go sleep with another woman so I can have a baby?"* Back in the day, having Hagar as a surrogate mother was acceptable to the culture, but just because the culture agrees with a decision, doesn't mean that God does!

Sarai just couldn't leave well enough alone, could she? She couldn't follow her husband and God's plan for her life. She took the lead and Abram agreed to what she said. (Genesis 16:2) Sarai was a wife of influence just like you and I, my friend!

Now here's the kicker to Sarai's story.... She blamed her husband for the mistreatment she was receiving by Hagar! Umm, and whose idea was it in the first place to sleep with Hagar? I'm glad I wasn't invited to their house for dinner when Sarai and Abram were having *that* conversation.
You know they were having some words, and if they had doors in their tent, they'd be slamming them too!

Oh girlfriend, sometimes we just make stupid decisions and we let some of our absurd emotions lead us. Poor Sarai, her discontentment, desperation, jealousy, and controlling plan backfired on her.

Of course Sarai became jealous of Hagar which caused Hagar to run away. Later Hagar came back, but you know there was strife in the home, especially when Sarai gave birth to Isaac. Ishmael had disdain for the new kid in the family (Genesis 21:9) which ticked Sarai off so she told Abram to cast them out from their home, and being that Sarai was a wife of influence, Abram did what Sarai wanted.

Here's something you'll find interesting. Because Abram did not follow God's promise, the two sons who birthed two nations (Israel and the Arab Nation) are still at odds with each other to this day, several thousand years later. One is the Jewish nation that came from Isaac, Sarai's son, and the other one is the Arab nation fathered by Ishmael, Hagar's son.

Women don't wear jealousy well. Nor do we wear manipulation and taking the lead of our homes. Sarai made a mess. How many times have we made a mess in our marriage? Times when we manipulate or try to control our husband only to have our situation become worse than what it already is?

Lessons to Learn from the Life of Sarai...

♥ Don't take the lead in your marriage. God has given the position of headship to your husband, so let him fill it.

♥ If you choose to go outside of the will of God, your life will be harder than what it is today. You will have consequences for your actions.

♥ This is a no-brainer... don't tell your man to sleep with another woman. Ever.

℘ Application ✍

When you're faced with difficulties in life, instead of taking control and telling your husband what to do, trust in God's plan for your life, instead.

Rather than becoming controlling in your situation, you can work at controlling your emotions and feelings. This is what I try to do, but sometimes I can't get a grip, so I will politely walk away and discuss matters at a time when I can pull myself together.

If you have a tendency to be controlling, bossy, demeaning, or demanding towards your man, then work at changing your behavior. Bite your tongue and keep your mouth shut if need be. You won't be perfect in this pursuit, no wife is, but God looks at your heart and He recognizes your motives.

Determine to let go of whatever issue is bothering you and give it to the Lord for Him to handle.

Lesson 4

The Discouraging Wife

She faced a lot of trials.

She lost her possessions, her cattle, wealth, home and even her children. And then her husband fell ill.

This couple lived through some depressing times.

In spite of all their horrendous trials, her husband did his best to follow the Lord. A Godly man he was, yet, his wife didn't care too much about that.

So who is this wife?

She's the wife of Job.

Here's her story…

"Do you still hold fast to your integrity? Curse God and die!" But he said to her, "You speak as one of the foolish women speaks. Shall we indeed accept good from God, and shall we not accept adversity?" In all this Job did not sin with his lips. Job 2:9, 10

There's not a whole lot written on Mrs. Job but we can still learn from her mistake. If you're facing some similar afflictions like Job and his wife try to remember that God has a plan for all that you're enduring. I know this is not easy and I'm saying this from first hand experience. I know what it's like to feel like you can't endure much more. And I know what it's like to feel forsaken by the Lord. I've lived through many years of heartache as I endured countless years of financial storms and chronic ill-health, however, God was and is always with us. I've seen His mighty hand time and time again in my life. You'll see it in your life, too. Look for Him to show up and perform miracles because He always does.

God knew that Job was going to sing praises to His name regardless of what the Lord took him through. He's doing the same with you too, my friend. Be a faithful, God-fearing wife and cling to Christ in the midst of adversities.

The testimony of Job's faithfulness has encouraged and ministered to countless saints throughout the ages. Be a willing vessel and let God use your testimony to minister to others as well.

This one perspective has helped me get through all of my pity-parties. I try to be intentional about building God's Kingdom rather than feeling sorry for myself when I can't build my own.

Lessons to Learn from the Life of Job's Wife...

♥ We will always have trials because we're not promised heaven on earth. But as a wife, never kick your husband while he's down. And if he's clinging to the Lord, praise him for that!

♥ Oh friend, I can't even begin to think about the anguish this mama must have felt when she lost her precious family. However, I do know one thing; never give up on following Christ! He is our hope, peace, joy, and strength. No believer, in ANY circumstance should encourage another person to pull away from the One True God.

♥ Don't be so earthly minded when living through gut-wrenching storms, instead, turn your eyes towards heaven; your eternal home. This eternal perspective will soothe not only your soul, but your husband's as well.

❧ Application ❧

Affirm your husband. Let your man know you're proud of him and you'll continue to stand by his side even in the midst of adversity, afflictions, heartache, and pain.

Have an attitude of gratitude when faced with financial turmoil.

He (Job) said, "I came naked from my mother's womb, and I will be naked when I leave. The LORD gave me what I had, and the LORD has taken it away. Praise the name of the LORD!" Job 1:21 (NLT)

Lesson 5

The Wife Who Despised Her Husband

This wife's marriage started off so promising.

The couple was young and in love! *Sound familiar?*

She couldn't wait to marry her man, but she was forced to wait because her father used her as a bargaining chip.

Finally the time came for when she was allowed to marry her dreamboat.

So who is this wife?

She's Michal, the wife of David before he became King.

Here's her story...

> Now Michal, Saul's daughter, loved David.
> And they told Saul, and the thing pleased him.
> 1 Samuel 18:20 Then Saul gave him Michal his
> daughter as a wife. Thus Saul saw and knew
> that the LORD was with David, and
> that Michal, Saul's daughter, loved him. 1
> Samuel 18:27,28

But then things changed for Michal. Her husband
became her father's biggest threat and enemy to his
kingdom. Michal started off as a good wife. She was
loyal to her man and helped save his life from her
own despicable father.

> Saul also sent messengers to David's house to
> watch him and to kill him in the morning.
> And Michal, David's wife, told him, saying, "If
> you do not save your life tonight, tomorrow
> you will be killed." So Michal let David down
> through a window. And he went and fled and
> escaped. 1 Samuel 19:11,12

But the two young lovers were broken apart. It was
during the time that David spent fleeing for his life
that Saul gave Michal over to another man in
marriage. *(Gee, thanks Dad.)*

> But Saul had given Michal his daughter,
> David's wife, to Palti the son of Laish, who was
> from Gallim. 1 Samuel 25:44

Many years later after Saul died, David is now King. David makes a covenant agreement to reign over all Israel, yet he requires one thing in order to do so. He wants his wife, Michal, back! Sounds romantic, doesn't it? Well, don't be fooled because it's not what you think!

> And David said, "Good, I will make a covenant with you. But one thing I require of you: you shall not see my face unless you first bring Michal, Saul's daughter, when you come to see my face." So David sent messengers to Ishbosheth, Saul's son, saying, "Give me my wife Michal, whom I betrothed to myself for a hundred foreskins of the Philistines." And Ishbosheth sent and took her from her husband, from Paltiel the son of Laish. Then her husband went along with her to Bahurim, weeping behind her. 2 Samuel 3:13-16

Michal's husband appeared to be brokenhearted over the fact that his wife was taken from him.

But regarding Michal's and David's love story this is what we know... They started off in love. Family meddled in their affairs and yes, that's putting it lightly when your own father seeks to kill your husband. Michal is then sent off to marry another man; a man who appears to love her deeply. I can't help but think she reciprocated those feeling based on how she later responds to David.

Let's take a look to see how this train-wreck of a love story unfolds.

The scene....

Michal is back at the palace and David just came home from bringing the Ark of the Covenant to the City of David. This was a big deal to the Israelites because now they could freely worship the Lord!

Let's find out if Michal is excited for her Godly husband's efforts?

> Now as the ark of the LORD came into the City of David, Michal, Saul's daughter, looked through a window and saw King David leaping and whirling before the LORD; and she despised him in her heart. 2 Samuel 6:16

Unfortunately, Michal wasn't impressed or supportive of her husband's endeavors. Not only was she not thrilled, but she despised him as well. Maybe her heart longed to be back with her other man? The Scriptures don't tell us these things but you can only wonder what went wrong between the two love birds.

But now Michal makes a bad situation even worse when she mocks David for his God-honoring behavior. Big mistake!

Then David returned to bless his household. And Michal the daughter of Saul came out to meet David, and said, "How glorious was the king of Israel today, uncovering himself today in the eyes of the maids of his servants, as one of the base fellows shamelessly uncovers himself!" So David said to Michal, "It was before the LORD, who chose me instead of your father and all his house, to appoint me ruler over the people of the LORD, over Israel. Therefore I will play music before the LORD. "And I will be even more undignified than this, and will be humble in my own sight. But as for the maidservants of whom you have spoken, by them I will be held in honor." 2 Sam. 6:20-22

I happen to love sarcasm. It's my absolute favorite type of humor, with animal humor coming in at close second! But I will say that using sarcasm as a putdown towards my husband (and vice versa) is something my man and I try not to do in our marriage. In reality, when you use sarcasm like this, it just tears the other person down.

I believe that David was just to blame for this messed up marriage. I think he took Michal back because of his pride. But instead of Michal embracing this situation and letting the Lord vindicate her, which I believe would have been extremely difficult for any woman to do, she responded by going to the complete opposite direction. She mocked King David for *praising the Lord*.

Michal's heart became so bitter towards a man she was once so deeply in love with but now she despises him and mocks him for praising the Lord. Wow, there's a great deal of hatred and bitterness in that woman's heart. Of course David was no angel in this situation either. I believe he was having a bad character moment day when he demanded to have Michal back as his wife. At the time he already had 4 other wives, did he really need to have her as well? Or was he just letting the people of the land know that he was now King by having Michal, Saul's daughter, as his wife again? The Scriptures don't say, but what we do know is that it didn't end well for Michal.

Therefore Michal the daughter of Saul had no children to the day of her death. 2 Samuel 6:23

Lessons to Learn from the Life of Michal...

♥ Michal started off in love with her husband just like most wives. She put her loyalty towards her husband before her father. Smart move on her part even in the midst of turmoil.

♥ She could have tried to make the best of her situation. I realize she had a lot of bad circumstances in her love life, but God is a great God who restores and redeems. Perhaps she could've tried to trust God rather than become bitter?

❤ Mocking a husband will never draw him closer to you nor will it strengthen your marriage.

♥ Application ♥

Whatever difficult circumstance you're dealing with in your marriage, hand it over to the Lord. Becoming bitter towards your husband or mocking him for his behavior will not solve your marital problems; it will only make your relationship worse.

Lay your marriage at the foot of the Cross and be willing to surrender your will to your Heavenly Father. Jesus makes all things new. Trust Him on this one and give Him some time to work in your life and in the life of your husband.

Looking to pull the weeds of bitterness out of your marriage? Start by forgiving your husband for some of the dumb things he has done in your marriage, after all, no one is perfect. We all do dumb things.

Lesson 6

The Worldly Wife

This wife makes me sad.

She lived in a desirable and luxurious land, but it was also extremely wicked.

God had a much better plan for her life than what she was capable of seeing.

The Lord was leading her and her family to a new place, but she didn't want to leave her home.

She wasn't willing to let go of her current lifestyle.

She longed for it as she looked back.

So who is this wife?

She's the wife of Lot.

Here's her story...

> Lot moved his tents to a place near Sodom and
> settled among the cities of the plain. But the
> people of this area were extremely wicked and
> constantly sinned against the LORD. Genesis
> 13:12,13 With the coming of dawn, the angels
> urged Lot, saying, "Hurry! Take your wife and
> your two daughters who are here, or you will
> be swept away when the city is punished."
> When he hesitated, the men grasped his hand
> and the hands of his wife and of his two
> daughters and led them safely out of the city,
> for the LORD was merciful to them. As soon
> as they had brought them out, one of them
> said, "Flee for your lives! Don't look back, and
> don't stop anywhere in the plain! Flee to the
> mountains or you will be swept away!"
> Genesis 19:15-17 Then the LORD rained down
> burning sulfur on Sodom and Gomorrah--from
> the LORD out of the heavens. Genesis 19:24
> But Lot's wife looked back, and she became a
> pillar of salt. Genesis 19:26

Money and possessions are two things that we're
always going to battle within our marriage. Our
fleshly desires scream, "I want it," or we fear the
future. If we continually turn to our flesh, a.k.a, our
emotions and feelings, then it will rob us of our joy
and cause us to bicker with our husband.

I once knew a woman who faced the loss of what she
once knew; home, car, and lifestyle.

But instead of trusting in God, she made the decision to leave her husband and child. She willingly chose to go outside of the will of God and divorce her husband because the financial strain she was living through was too much for her to bear.

Lessons to Learn from the Life of Lot's Wife...

♥ Don't become so consumed with your current lifestyle that you're not willing to follow the Lord where ever He sends you. Remember, this place on earth is just your temporary home.

♥ Don't place a higher emphasis on money over your husband and family. Be mindful of this thought-process when the arguments over finances start to break out in your home.

♥ If and when God moves you, don't look back. Reach for the things that are ahead.

Forgetting those things which are behind and reaching forward to those things which are ahead, I press toward the goal for the prize of the upward call of God in Christ Jesus. Phil. 3:13-14

❧ Application ❧

If financial concerns are weighing down your wedded union, keep this perspective:

For where your treasure is, there your heart will be also.
Matthew 6:21

Treasure your marriage more then your possessions. Let your man know you'd follow him to a soup kitchen if need be.

Lesson 7

The Manipulative Wife

She was an adulterous.

She had a man thrown in prison.

She later wanted him killed.

She collaborated with her teen-aged daughter to have her dance seductively for her husband. *What mother does that?*

So who is this wife?

She's Herodias, King Herod's wife.

In my book, this wife is a piece of work. She was once married to Phillip, King Herod's half-brother, but King Herod was more prominent than Phillip, so Philip got kicked to the curb.

Herodias was seeking a higher status in life than what Phillip was able to give her so she decided to hook up with, and marry Philip's half-brother, Herod of Antipas. But there was one problem with her gold-digger plan, and his name was John the Baptist. This eccentric and bold prophet called them out in their sin. The truth that John the Baptist spoke regarding their lives went over like a led balloon in the eyes of Herodias. Putting it more bluntly, John the Baptist's words infuriated her. So Herodias did what any wife in her adulterous position would do... she demanded that John be put in jail regardless of how her husband felt about him.

Here's her story...

> For Herod himself had sent and laid hold of John, and bound him in prison for the sake of Herodias, his brother Philip's wife; for he had married her. Because John had said to Herod, "It is not lawful for you to have your brother's wife." Therefore Herodias held it against him and wanted to kill him, but she could not; for Herod feared John, knowing that he was a just and holy man, and he protected him. And when he heard him, he did many things, and heard him gladly. Mark 6:17-20

At first glance, we may not personally relate to Herodias' choices, because, well, it's not too often that we marry one man only to divorce him and then marry *his brother* and then go so far as to murder a person because we didn't like what they had to say about us!

But like any wife, Herodias had influence over her husband and she knew her husband's weaknesses. Her man was filled with pride. All husbands have pride and if it's not kept in check it can cause just about any man to stumble. Remember Vashti's man? He fell way to his pride when he hastily banished Vashti from his kingdom. He actually later regretted his decision because he missed her.

Anyways, back to Herodias…

> Then an opportune day came when Herod on his birthday gave a feast for his nobles, the high officers, and the chief men of Galilee. And when Herodias' daughter herself came in and danced, and pleased Herod and those who sat with him, the king said to the girl, "Ask me whatever you want, and I will give it to you." He also swore to her, "Whatever you ask me, I will give you, up to half my kingdom." Immediately she came in with haste to the king and asked, saying, "I want you to give me at once the head of John the Baptist on a platter." And the king was exceedingly sorry; yet, because of the oaths and because of those who sat with him, he did not want to refuse her. Immediately the king sent an executioner and commanded his head to be brought. And he went and beheaded him in prison, brought his head on a platter, and gave it to the girl; and the girl gave it to her mother. Mark 6:21-28

Herodias had her own agenda. She sought to bring glory to herself and she wanted to satisfy the desires of her flesh. She was manipulative and she was going to do whatever it took to get what she wanted.

> With narrowed eyes, people plot evil;
> with a smirk, they plan their mischief.
> Prov. 16:30 NLT

Definition of manipulate:
To influence someone, or to control something, in a clever or dishonest way.

As Believers, we never need to manipulate a person or a situation. Our King of Kings is seated on throne. He knows all things and He's always a part of every equation in our lives. He's got our backs, therefore, we can safely rest in Him and the plans He has for us. We don't need to stir the pot, position ourselves, or try to manipulate a situation. Our purpose as a God-fearing wife is to have our marriage reflect Christ and the Church. We can simply rest and trust God with every ounce of our marriage.

When we seek to take the path of manipulating our husband, we are essentially doing three things:

1. We're not trusting God with our circumstances.

2. We're not looking out for our husband's best interest.

3. We're seeking to have our desires fulfilled, whether it be lusts of the flesh (things we want) or we're seeking to control a situation due to our fears and/or our pride.

If you look at all three of these paths, not one of them leads us to a closer relationship with Jesus Christ.

Manipulation doesn't help us to trust Christ more.

Manipulation does not strengthen our marital union.

And manipulation doesn't help us as Believers to lay down our lives. It does all of the opposite here. Manipulation is a cancer to any marriage. It's poisonous and toxic.

Lessons to Learn from the Life of Herodias...

♥ She exercised zero self-control.

> Better to be patient than powerful; better to have self-control than to conquer a city. Proverbs 16:32 NLT

♥ She was consumed with self.

> I say then: Walk in the Spirit, and you shall not fulfill the lust of the flesh. Galatians 5:16

♥ She was discontent with her life. She wanted more than what she had and she manipulated others to get her way.

Regardless of the potential ramifications you may face in life, speak the truth, anyways.   I'm sure John the Baptist did not regret the fact that he was imprisoned and then beheaded for speaking the truth. He went to be with the Lord all because he proclaimed God's message whether people wanted to hear it or not. We would do well to follow the footsteps of such a bold, awe-inspiring, and God-fearing man.

৯৯ Application ৯৯

Seek to be a wife of integrity and honor, one who is intentional about making sure your plans are in line with the Lord's plans.

Don't manipulate your man to get what you want. Your self-centered ways can have a negative impact on others.

Lesson 8

The Wife Who Placed a Higher Priority on Her Mothering vs. Her Marriage

If you have children, then you'll most likely relate to this wife on some level.

She was one busy lady raising two rambunctious boys; so rambunctious she felt like a battle was taking place within her womb while she was pregnant. Yes, she was carrying twins.

She made some poor decisions as she raised them, so much so, that her favorite son followed her deceptive ways.

She showed more loyalty toward her offspring than to her husband.

So who is this wife?

She's Rebekah, Isaac's wife.

I can understand how Rebekah lost sight of her marriage, after all, as moms, we spend so much time with our children that it's simple for us to become more attached to our kids than our man. But before we look at the wrong choices Rebekah made in her marriage, first we need to see where she went wrong in her parenting.

Here's her story…

> Isaac pleaded with the LORD on behalf of his wife, because she was unable to have children. The LORD answered Isaac's prayer, and Rebekah became pregnant with twins. But the two children struggled with each other in her womb. So she went to ask the LORD about it. "Why is this happening to me?" she asked. And the LORD told her, "The sons in your womb will become two nations. From the very beginning, the two nations will be rivals. One nation will be stronger than the other; and your older son will serve your younger son."
> And when the time came to give birth, Rebekah discovered that she did indeed have twins!

The first one was very red at birth and covered with thick hair like a fur coat. So they named him Esau. Then the other twin was born with his hand grasping Esau's heel. So they named him Jacob. Isaac was sixty years old when the twins were born. As the boys grew up, Esau became a skillful hunter. He was an outdoorsman, but Jacob had a quiet temperament, preferring to stay at home. Isaac loved Esau because he enjoyed eating the wild game Esau brought home, but Rebekah loved Jacob. Genesis 25:21-28

Rebekah played favorites. (So did Isaac, but in this book I'm talking about wives.)

Now on to Rebekah's marriage mistake...

One day when Isaac was old and turning blind, he called for Esau, his older son, and said, "My son." "Yes, Father?" Esau replied. "I am an old man now," Isaac said, "and I don't know when I may die. Take your bow and a quiver full of arrows, and go out into the open country to hunt some wild game for me. Prepare my favorite dish, and bring it here for me to eat. Then I will pronounce the blessing that belongs to you, my firstborn son, before I die." But Rebekah overheard what Isaac had said to his son Esau. So when Esau left to hunt for the wild game, she said to her son Jacob, "Listen. I overheard your father say to Esau, 'Bring me some wild game and prepare me a delicious meal.

Then I will bless you in the LORD's presence before I die.' Now, my son, listen to me. Do exactly as I tell you. Go out to the flocks, and bring me two fine young goats. I'll use them to prepare your father's favorite dish. Genesis 27:1-9

Rebekah purposefully deceived her own husband and she encouraged her son to do the same thing. She chose to have a deeper relationship with her son over her man. I know this is a marriage book, but I'm going to mix in some parenting thoughts so we can gain a better perspective on Rebekah's wrong choices. Seeing how I'm a 'why' kind of gal, meaning, I like to know 'why' did Rebekah's mothering take precedence over her marriage, we're going to dig into the root issue of her problem.

The verse below will shed some light on to why we moms do what we do; why we move closer towards our kids than our husband.

Remember the consequence that Eve received from God in Genesis 3:16? Well, there were two parts to it. One part was that Eve, and you and I will want to control our husband, and the second part relates to mothering.

Let's take a look at the Scriptures…
> To the woman He said: "I will greatly multiply your sorrow and your conception; in pain you shall bring forth children. Genesis 3:16

We generally just look at the verse as having pain *during* childbirth, but there's much more to it than that. Notice that the verse does not say a baby, it says *children*. You are raising up kids. Kids that require so much from you. Kids that need constant training. Kids that can set you over the edge and bring you to your knees. Kids that are sinners. I have a few of them in my home so I can relate to all of this!

Our struggle isn't just in the birthing of the babes; it's also in the raising of them. Let me ask you a mom question. Do you ever feel like you've done enough for your kiddos? Feel like you've got everything covered in the mom department? I already know your answer because it's the same as mine. We *know* we fall short in our mothering and that's why we have the mommy guilt. This struggle is what makes it so easy for us to be lopsided in our family relationships; investing more of ourselves into our mothering vs. our marriage. And of course it's much easier to become emotionally connected to a child who makes you feel unconditionally loved. Also, our children don't hurt us or let us down nearly as much as our husband, thus, it's easier to draw closer to our kids.

Motherhood and Marriage is not about balance, it's about prioritizing. I know we hear the word balance all the time, but instead of seeking balance, look to change your perspective just slightly. Prioritize instead, and I think this viewpoint will help you to not feel so overwhelmed in all of your roles and responsibilities.

Lessons to Learn from the Life of Rebekah...

♥ Don't view your role as a mother as more important than your role as a wife because this is not the proper biblical order. I know it's so easy to place a higher priority upon motherhood especially when you've got little tykes all around you or even if you're homeschooling. Kids take time to nurture and train. Young children require a great amount of energy from mama. I'm certainly not discounting the role of motherhood as I share with you about this wife- not at all! I'm just saying it's easy to lose sight of your marital relationship because you're so busy parenting. Someday your children will leave your nest and cleave to a family of their own.

♥ Don't take on the role of parenting all by yourself. Let your husband become involved as much as possible, even if he doesn't do things the way you do. Having him dress your adorable toddler in striped shorts and a plaid shirt for church really is no big deal!

♥ Don't place your relationship with your children above your marriage. Work to become more emotionally connected to your man more so than your children.

♥ Love and treat each child the same. Don't have a favorite child.

- ♥ Be mindful of the fact that you are one flesh with your husband, not your children. I know it certainly doesn't feel that way when you're pregnant and nursing, but as Godly wives, we heed God's Word, not our feelings and emotions.

ᔓ Application ᔕ

Be intentional about making time to date your spouse. This doesn't have to be fancy or expensive. It's just a time set aside for you to reconnect with your husband. In my home we haven't had the funds to go out to dinner in quite sometime, so instead we stay home and put the kids to bed earlier so we can have some alone time.

If you're raising your kids in Christ, then you should be preparing your kids to be self-sufficient. If and when they marry, the correct biblical encouragement when taking a spouse is for your offspring to leave and cleave; leaving not just your home, but attaching themselves physically, emotionally, mentally, and spiritually to their spouse more so than you. I know you probably just felt a sharp knife being inserted into your mama's heart right now but those are God's plans, not mine!

On a side note: Let me give you a little glimpse into some additional messed up parenting from Rebekah's lineage.

If you go back into Rebekah's family you'll see that her brother is Laban. Laban is the father of Rachel and Leah. Rebekah's son, Jacob, whom she favored, married Rachel but Laban deceived him and he ended up marrying Leah instead. Jacob was heartbroken because of the love he had for Rachel. So Jacob decided to work another 7 years for Laban so he could then marry Rachel. Deception and favoritism runs through this family tree.

But wait, there's more. Do you know or remember the story about Joseph and his brothers who threw him in a pit? Joseph's brothers did this because their father favored Joseph and thus, his brothers despised him. Do you know who Joseph's father was? If you guessed Jacob, you're right!

Make an effort to take a different path of mothering than the path that Rebekah chose.

Lesson 9

The Lying and Prideful Wife

This wife unfortunately followed her lying husband's lead.

She was too proud to say she held some money back as her and her man chose not to give the Apostles all the profits from their land.

She was hoping the Believers would think she was more spiritually mature than what she truly was.

So who is this wife?

She's Sapphira, wife of Ananias.

Here's her story…
> But there was a certain man named Ananias who, with his wife, Sapphira, sold some property.

He brought part of the money to the apostles, claiming it was the full amount. With his wife's consent, he kept the rest. Then Peter said, "Ananias, why have you let Satan fill your heart? You lied to the Holy Spirit, and you kept some of the money for yourself. The property was yours to sell or not sell, as you wished. And after selling it, the money was also yours to give away. How could you do a thing like this? You weren't lying to us but to God!" As soon as Ananias heard these words, he fell to the floor and died. Everyone who heard about it was terrified. Then some young men got up, wrapped him in a sheet, and took him out and buried him. About three hours later his wife came in, not knowing what had happened. Peter asked her, "Was this the price you and your husband received for your land?" "Yes," she replied, "that was the price." And Peter said, "How could the two of you even think of conspiring to test the Spirit of the Lord like this? The young men who buried your husband are just outside the door, and they will carry you out, too." Instantly, she fell to the floor and died. When the young men came in and saw that she was dead, they carried her out and buried her beside her husband. Acts 5:1-10 (NLT)

Sometimes it's not easy knowing when to follow our husband and when not to. Sapphira was faced with this choice. But Sapphira was God's gal first before she was a wife to Ananias. Just like you and me.

Our allegiance and loyalty is with the Lord first, then our husband. I get countless emails from wives all around the world telling me of the dumb, sinful things their man wants them to submit to. Sure, God wants us to submit to our husband, but not to his sin. Submitting to his sin is not biblical and here's why:

Your sinful actions will bring dishonor to the Lord's name, not to mention, cause your husband to be at odds with his Maker.

Lessons to Learn from the Life of Sapphira…

- ♥ Don't follow your husband's lead when he is in sin. Period!

- ♥ Don't lie to the Holy Spirit.

- ♥ Don't try to prove to others that you're better or more spiritual than you really are. Be humble and rest in the Lord's strength. Others will appreciate your realness, and your husband will thank you for not competing and comparing yourself with others. Just be you, and let the Lord grow you spiritually in His time.

- ♥ What Sapphira could have done…She could have respectfully and graciously told her husband that she didn't want to lie to the Apostles. If her husband wanted to deceive them, then that was his choice *and his sin*. God will hold him accountable for his actions.

♥ She could have been content with where she was in her spiritual growth. Accepting who she was in Jesus Christ would have helped her not need the approval or praises from others.

Our purpose is to please God, not people. He alone examines the motives of our hearts. 1 Thes. 2:4 NLT

---

୨ Application ୧

Be honorable and truthful to your husband. Your integrity may actually rub off on him if his character needs to grow in this area. Remember, you are a wife of influence. Spur your guy on towards righteousness.

Lesson 10

The Unfaithful Wife

She's a seductress.

She's a tempter.

She's a liar.

So who is this wife?

She's Potiphar's wife.

Here's her story…

> So Potiphar gave Joseph complete administrative responsibility over everything he owned. With Joseph there, he didn't worry about a thing—except what kind of food to eat!

Joseph was a very handsome and well-built young man, and Potiphar's wife soon began to look at him lustfully. "Come and sleep with me," she demanded. But Joseph refused. "Look," he told her, "my master trusts me with everything in his entire household. No one here has more authority than I do. He has held back nothing from me except you, because you are his wife. How could I do such a wicked thing? It would be a great sin against God." She kept putting pressure on Joseph day after day, but he refused to sleep with her, and he kept out of her way as much as possible. One day, however, no one else was around when he went in to do his work. She came and grabbed him by his cloak, demanding, "Come on, sleep with me!" Joseph tore himself away, but he left his cloak in her hand as he ran from the house. When she saw that she was holding his cloak and he had fled, she called out to her servants. Soon all the men came running. "Look!" she said. "My husband has brought this Hebrew slave here to make fools of us! He came into my room to rape me, but I screamed. When he heard me scream, he ran outside and got away, but he left his cloak behind with me." She kept the cloak with her until her husband came home. Then she told him her story. "That Hebrew slave you've brought into our house tried to come in and fool around with me," she said. "But when I screamed, he ran outside, leaving his cloak with me!"

Potiphar was furious when he heard his wife's story about how Joseph had treated her. So he took Joseph and threw him into the prison where the king's prisoners were held, and there he remained. Genesis 39:6-20

Apparently Potiphar's wife couldn't control herself when she caught a glimpse of Joseph. I guess he was easy on the eyes. Wow, this woman was brazen to say the least. The audacity she had to put sexual pressure on a man every single day just blows my mind. And then to top off her ridiculous pursuit, she demanded that Joseph sleep with her. This woman had some real issues. And let's not forget her deceitful actions when she lied about the whole incident and then had an innocent man thrown in jail.

So what can we learn from this woman, I mean, it's not like you and I are going to demand some other man to sleep with us, right?

Here's our connection to her...

Her story starts with lust. I believe every woman has a certain amount of lust running through her veins; whether it's a sexual lust towards another man or the lust of possessions or status. We all have some form of this sin. And because we're married, we naturally bring this sin straight into our marriage. We could be pushing our husband to make more money so we can live in our dream home.

Or we can pursue an inappropriate relationship with

the opposite sex because we're lusting after an emotional or sexual connection.

Bottom line is this: lust is just a form of discontentment. It's 'the grass is greener on the other side' syndrome. If you let this syndrome take root in your marriage, then your marriage will not flourish when you go through life with a discontented perspective.

For all that is in the world--the lust of the flesh, the lust of the eyes, and the pride of life--is not of the Father but is of the world. 1 John 2:16

Lessons to Learn from the Life of Potiphar's Wife...

❤ Learn to be content with the life that God has given you.

❤ Seek out the blessings from above because if you look close enough, you will find them.

❤ Realize that every marriage needs to be watered. A relationship doesn't just naturally flourish. You need to give it proper care and attention just like you did when you and your man were dating and engaged.

❧ Application ❦

Learn to be a wife who is not of this world. Here are 4 simple ways to help you in this pursuit:

- Be intentional about reading the Word of God on a daily basis.
- Faithfully attend church each week.
- Surround yourself with Believers who will encourage you to grow in the Lord.
- Serve the Lord with your spiritual gifts.

A word to the wife who has been unfaithful,

If you're repentant for your past sins, then God has washed you as white as snow. You are forgiven and redeemed by the blood of the Lamb. Don't listen to the Enemy as he tries to condemn you for your past mistakes. If you do, then he'll rob you of your joy and the fullness of life that you have in Jesus Christ.

Lesson 11

The Bitter Wife

There was a famine in her country.

She followed her husband to a new land.

While there, her husband died.

Her sons married foreign wives, but later her sons died too.

So who is this wife?

She's Naomi, the wife of Elimelech.

Here's her story...

> Now it came to pass, in the days when the judges ruled, that there was a famine in the land.

And a certain man of Bethlehem, Judah, went to dwell in the country of Moab, he and his wife and his two sons. The name of the man was Elimelech, the name of his wife was Naomi, and the names of his two sons were Mahlon and Chilion--Ephrathites of Bethlehem, Judah. And they went to the country of Moab and remained there. Then Elimelech, Naomi's husband, died; and she was left, and her two sons. Now they took wives of the women of Moab: the name of the one was Orpah, and the name of the other Ruth. And they dwelt there about ten years. Then both Mahlon and Chilion also died; so the woman survived her two sons and her husband. Ruth 1:1-5

Initially, I wasn't going to write on Naomi's life when I first started writing this book. I only saw Naomi as a bitter woman who was now a widow. I couldn't see how she would be relatable to us. But the Lord pressed upon my heart (more than once) that I needed to go back and read more about this woman. After learning about her and what the Lord revealed to me, I can now truly say that I think *every* wife in some way will relate to Naomi even if you're not a widow.

Let's find out about this wife, shall we?

As I mentioned earlier, Naomi is now a widow living in the foreign land of Moab, which is now facing a famine as well.

Because of the financial turmoil that she's living in, she decides to head back to her home, the land of Judah. She tells her daughter-in-laws to head back to their mother's house and to remarry, but one daughter-in-law, Ruth, is pretty darn obstinate and is unwilling to leave Naomi's side. I believe Naomi left quite a mark on this young woman's life if she was so willing to follow Naomi and leave her own homeland.

Then they lifted up their voices and wept again; and Orpah kissed her mother-in-law, but Ruth clung to her. And she said, "Look, your sister-in-law has gone back to her people and to her gods; return after your sister-in-law." But Ruth said: "Entreat me not to leave you, or to turn back from following after you; For wherever you go, I will go; And wherever you lodge, I will lodge; Your people shall be my people, And your God, my God. Where you die, I will die, and there will I be buried. The LORD do so to me, and more also, if anything but death parts you and me." Ruth 1:12-17

Ruth must have loved Naomi tremendously to follow her anywhere and for her to proclaim that Naomi's God would be her God. Naomi must have faithfully ministered to Ruth despite the heartache and despair that Naomi lived through. It's one thing to feel forsaken and bitter towards God but it's something all together very different when your walk draws people to your Lord.

Now the two of them went until they came to Bethlehem. And it happened, when they had come to Bethlehem, that all the city was excited because of them; and the women said, "Is this Naomi?" But she said to them, "Do not call me Naomi; call me Mara, for the Almighty has dealt very bitterly with me. "I went out full, and the LORD has brought me home again empty. Why do you call me Naomi, since the LORD has testified against me, and the Almighty has afflicted me?" Ruth 1:19-21

Did you know the name Mara means bitter? I got a kick out of Naomi's raw honesty and emotions. In some ways I can relate to her bitterness. For most of my marriage I have lived in a constant state of trials. In fact, I think 'trial' is a regular member of our household, and he never wants to leave. At one point in my life my husband and I moved 4 times in an 18-month period. These were not fun and exciting moves, by the way, they were depressing and exhausting. They left me wondering where God was in the midst of my suffering. They left me questioning my faith. They left me with fear of the unknown. And they left me feeling more like I worked at a moving company rather than feeling like my husband's wife, and one day I told my husband just that. With tears falling down my face, I said to my man, *"I don't feel like your wife anymore. I feel like the housekeeper going from one home to the next, cleaning and packing, then cleaning and unpacking. I'm exhausted and worn-out and I feel like our marriage is drowning in all of these storms."*

I hesitated to share any of this with my Beloved because I could tell he was exhausted as well. I didn't want to bring him down in anyway and I didn't want to discourage him anymore than what he was already feeling. Not only was he exhausted, but he was a broken man; a man, who once provided so well for his family was now reduced to having us live temporarily with friends and then moving us from one place to another. He was broken in every sense of the word.

I wrestled with God *often* over all the trials He allowed in our lives. We were intentional about trying to live honorable lives seeking to bring God glory in all we did. We sought to lift His name on high. To walk out the Biblical commands of loving and respecting one another. To raise up Godly offspring. To be His hands and feet to others. And yet, we were faced with one storm after another in our marriage.

I didn't understand why God took us through so much hardship but I knew I still had to hold on to God's Word in spite of our circumstances. One reminder I hold close to my heart when I'm living through great anguish and immense pain is this verse Peter said to Jesus, *"Lord, to whom shall we go? You have the words of eternal life." John 6:68*

I think Naomi had a similar viewpoint. She still put one foot in front of the other and followed the Lord regardless of her feelings.

Naomi eventually led her daughter-in-law, Ruth, to her future husband, Boaz, who was a part of Naomi's husband's lineage. Ruth and Boaz birthed a child, named Obed, who became the father of Jesse, who fathered David who became the King of Israel. Jesus, the Messiah, came through this blood line and I believe the Lord honored Naomi for her devotion and obedience to Him.

It's easy to read how Naomi's life unfolds and the good that came out of it because we see the big picture. However, that's not our situation. We only see our past and present circumstances. We don't know how God is going to work things out in our lives, but we have to trust that He will.

Lessons to Learn from the Life of Naomi...

- ♥ Regardless of Naomi's dire and depressing circumstances and the emotions that welled up within her heart, Naomi stilled faithfully followed the Lord.

- ♥ She stood on the Truth of who God is rather than allowing her feelings to dictate her choices. Yes, there will be times in our lives where our emotions will over take our hearts just like they took up residence in Naomi's, but Naomi didn't allow her feelings to govern her decisions. Naomi walked in Truth even though her feelings screamed the exact opposite.

- In spite of Naomi's heartache and pain, she sought to serve others when she helped Ruth marry Boaz. She ultimately took her eyes of off herself and her pain.

- Naomi didn't have her husband to help her walk through the pain of her life, but you and I do. Fight the good fight with your man instead of fighting against him.

♥ Application ♥

1. Keep walking *The Narrow Path* no matter how grueling life gets. You never know who's watching you and the impact your witness may have on the lives of those around you.

2. Don't let your trials become idols within your marriage. When you're constantly focusing on them, it can suck the life right out of your love and passion for one another. (And, dwelling on your trials will leave you in a defeated, spiritual state. Not that I'd know anything about this!)

3. Avoid complacency in your marriage and be on guard because the Enemy is roaming the earth, to and fro, seeking whom he can devour. He'd love to destroy your marriage, so don't give him a foothold.

4. Change your perspective about your trials. Look at them as an opportunity to grow closer to the Lord and to your husband.

5. Remain in fellowship with other Believers. When you're empty and weary, the Body of Christ can minister to you.

6. Remain in God's Word so you can be encouraged, strengthened and comforted by the *Great I Am*. This will help you to not turn inward and throw that pity party we all love to throw, and it'll give you the ability to pour into your spouse when he needs to be lifted up.

7. Make the best of your situation. This is your life, your marriage, and your family, be thankful for what God has given you. Laugh. Be creative with your resources (if they're strained.) Help others, like Naomi did.

8. Read the Word of God to one another. If one spouse happens to be spiritually encouraged one day, they can read the Word to the one who is discouraged. My husband and I did this often in our marriage and I can say that out of all the years of trials that we faced there were only a handful of days that we were both downcast together.

9. When you're faced with one trial after another, meditate on the following verse so you can have a heavenly perspective in the midst of your suffering.

Therefore we do not lose heart. Even though our outward man is perishing, yet the inward man is being renewed day by day. For our light affliction, which is but for a moment, is working for us a far more exceeding and eternal weight of glory, while we do not look at the things which are seen, but at the things which are not seen. For the things which are seen are temporary, but the things which are not seen are eternal. 2 Corinthians 4:16-18

10. When your emotions start to dictate your life, will you seek to lean into the One who gives you peace? Will you keep your mind on the Lord? Or on your circumstances?

You will keep him in perfect peace, whose mind is stayed on You, because he trusts in You. Isaiah 26:3

11. Trials will either leave you feeling bitter or better. Which path will you choose?

Lesson 12

The Unloved Wife

She was an unwanted wife.

Her husband wasn't attracted to her.

Her man loved another woman.

So who is this wife?

She's Leah, Jacob's wife.

Here's her story…

> Now Laban had two daughters: the name of
> the elder was Leah, and the name of the
> younger was Rachel. Leah's eyes were
> delicate, but Rachel was beautiful of form and
> appearance.

Now Jacob loved Rachel; so he said, "I will serve you seven years for Rachel your younger daughter." Genesis 29:16-18 So Jacob served seven years for Rachel, and they seemed only a few days to him because of the love he had for her. Then Jacob said to Laban, "Give me my wife, for my days are fulfilled, that I may go in to her." Gen. 29:21 Now it came to pass in the evening, that he took Leah his daughter and brought her to Jacob; and he went in to her. Gen. 29:23 So it came to pass in the morning, that behold, it was Leah. And he said to Laban, "What is this you have done to me? Was it not for Rachel that I served you? Why then have you deceived me?" Gen. 29:25

Poor Leah, I can't even imagine being in her situation. What must have been going through her mind when her father had her marry her sister's guy? And then to have her new husband wake up in the morning and find out the truth about the whole situation! She was instantly rejected, and on her wedding night, no less!

Now most likely you have a monogamous marriage like mine! We are not sharing our husband with another wife, so you might be wondering how on earth can we relate to this wife? Well, we can, so hang with me.

Here's the root issue to Leah's hurting heart...

Her husband didn't meet her needs. Now do you see it? Do you see how relatable her story really is to our lives? Leah's husband placed his affection elsewhere. In this case, Jacob gave his affection to Rachel, another woman. But any man can so easily place his affection and attention on things other than his wife.

Perhaps it's his business.

His career.

His hobbies.

His children.

Maybe he's consumed with fears, finances, stress.

Perhaps he's dealing with an illness.

It can be any number of things.

Having a husband's attention and affection shift from the wife in a marriage is a pretty common thing. But because Leah's marriage starts off bad, she tries to win her husband's love. No wife could blame her for her motive.

> When the LORD saw that Leah was unloved, He opened her womb; but Rachel was barren. Gen. 29:31

The Lord blesses her with a child, then another, then another.

Each time she gets pregnant she's hoping she'll win Jacob over and then he'll be smitten with her, instead of Rachel. But each time a child is conceived in Leah, nothing changes in Jacob's heart towards her.

> She conceived again and bore a son, and said, "Now this time my husband will become attached to me, because I have borne him three sons." Therefore his name was called Levi.

And then one day Leah got it. She had an 'a-ha' moment. She realized her worth was in the Lord and that the Lord loved her!

> And she conceived again and bore a son, and said, "Now I will praise the LORD." Therefore she called his name Judah. Gen. 29:34,35

Every wife would do well to emulate Leah in the pursuit of praising our Lord rather than seeking the praises of our husband.

Lessons to Learn from the Life of Leah...

- ❤ Leah learned she couldn't change her husband's heart. Only the Holy Spirit can change a man's heart.

- ❤ She had to figure out how to go through life with her insecurities.

♥ She ultimately learned that her worth came from the Lord.

ᵞᵒ Application ᵒᵞ

Is there a disconnect in your relationship with your husband? Perhaps you're wanting to have a tighter bond with him? Here are 6 ways to help the two of you draw closer together.

1. Be his friend.

2. Take an interest in what he's interested in. Generally, men are not drawn to a woman's interest, so seek to move towards your man in the areas of his interest.

3. Ask him questions. Be involved with his life.

4. Have interests outside of just the parenting of your children.

5. If he's a believer, pray together.

6. Serve in ministry together.

Lesson 13

The Wife Who Cried Out to God

Her body was broken.

Her dreams were shattered.

Life wasn't going according to her plan.

Her husband's love wasn't enough to satisfy her.

So who is this wife?

She's Hannah, wife of Elkanah.

Here's her story....
> And he had two wives: the name of one was Hannah, and the name of the other Peninnah.

Peninnah had children, but Hannah had no children. This man went up from his city yearly to worship and sacrifice to the LORD of hosts in Shiloh. Also the two sons of Eli, Hophni and Phinehas, the priests of the LORD, were there. And whenever the time came for Elkanah to make an offering, he would give portions to Peninnah his wife and to all her sons and daughters. But to Hannah he would give a double portion, for he loved Hannah, although the LORD had closed her womb. And her rival also provoked her severely, to make her miserable, because the LORD had closed her womb. So it was, year by year, when she went up to the house of the LORD, that she provoked her; therefore she wept and did not eat. Then Elkanah her husband said to her, "Hannah, why do you weep? Why do you not eat? And why is your heart grieved? Am I not better to you than ten sons?" So Hannah arose after they had finished eating and drinking in Shiloh. Now Eli the priest was sitting on the seat by the doorpost of the tabernacle of the LORD. And she was in bitterness of soul, and prayed to the LORD and wept in anguish. Then she made a vow and said, "O LORD of hosts, if You will indeed look on the affliction of Your maidservant and remember me, and not forget Your maidservant, but will give Your maidservant a male child, then I will give him to the LORD all the days of his life, and no razor shall come upon his head." And it happened, as she continued praying before the LORD, that Eli watched her mouth. Now Hannah spoke in her heart; only her lips moved, but her voice was not heard. Therefore Eli thought she was drunk. So Eli said to her, "How long will you be drunk? Put your wine away from you!" But Hannah answered and said, "No, my lord, I am a woman of sorrowful spirit. I have drunk neither wine nor intoxicating drink, but have poured out my soul before the LORD. "Do not consider your maidservant a wicked woman, for out of the abundance of my complaint and grief I have spoken until now." Then Eli answered and said, "Go in peace, and the God of Israel grant your petition which you have asked of Him." And she said, "Let your maidservant find favor in your sight." So the woman went her way and ate, and her face was no longer sad. Then they rose early in the morning and worshiped before the LORD, and returned and came to their house at Ramah. And Elkanah knew Hannah his wife, and the LORD remembered her. So it came to pass in the process of time that Hannah conceived and bore a son, and called his name Samuel, saying, "Because I have asked for him from the LORD." 1 Samuel 1:2-20

I can relate to Hannah's pain, not necessarily her barrenness, but rather her body's brokenness and the bitterness that accompanied my soul like it accompanied Hannah's. I've got a very close and intimate relationship with emotional and physical pain due to the fact that I lived with chronic illnesses for over a decade. In fact, you could call us good friends. So I get Hannah's anguish, so much anguish that a priest would think she's drunk because she's beyond broken as she's uttering another petition to her Lord. I understand the weakness behind that prayer, as well as the hope it's coupled with.

Hannah desperately wanted a certain life but her body just wouldn't respond. The gal cried out to God, *often*. But nothing changed in her life, at least not in the physical world as we know it. But she was persistent in prayer. She wouldn't give up. She pressed in as she boldly went before the throne of God bringing her petitions to Him, year in and year out.

Maybe your body isn't working the way you'd like. Or perhaps you're barren or you're living with some chronic health conditions. Please know that you're not alone. God has a purpose in all that you're going through, just like He had a purpose for Hannah's life. Had Hannah been able to conceive like all the other wives, do you think she would have been so willing to offer up her boy to the Lord? We don't know that answer but we can see from Hannah's deepest pain and grief how God used her trial for His glory.

God uses our inabilities and our greatest sufferings so that the works of God might be displayed through us.

An example of this is the story of the blind man that Jesus ministered to.

> As he went along, he saw a man blind from birth. His disciples asked him, "Rabbi, who sinned, this man or his parents, that he was born blind?" "Neither this man nor his parents sinned," said Jesus, "but this happened so that the works of God might be displayed in him. John 9:1-3 (NIV)

Sometimes in our own brokenness we lose sight of how our storms and trials will work to bring glory to God. We can't see the purpose behind it but we can trust God with His plans for our lives.

And we know that all things work together for good to those who love God, to those who are the called according to His purpose. Romans 8:28

Lessons to Learn from the Life of Hannah....

- ♥ Even though she had a very loving husband, she knew her husband couldn't fix her problem. Husbands are not designed to be our Savior; this role is reserved for only One, Jesus Christ.

- ♥ There are certain aspects of a wife's life that can only be touched by our Father's hands. Hannah learned this wise lesson as she ran to her Father.

- ♥ She was patient, yet persistent in prayer.

♥ She made her life about honoring and pleasing the Lord rather than about herself.

❧ Application ❧

Thoughts for you to ponder…

- Do you trust God to work out your trials for His good and His purpose? Or for your good and your purpose?

- In the midst of your suffering are you persistent in prayer?

- Are you expecting your husband to save you from your suffering and anguish?

- Or are you putting your heartache in your Comforter's hands?

Be joyful in hope, patient in affliction, faithful in prayer.
Romans 12:12

Lesson 14

The Redeemed Wife

She had been married before, although not just once, but rather five different times.

The man she was currently living with was not her husband.

So who is this wife?

She's the Woman at the Well.

Here's her story...

> "Please, sir," the woman said, "give me this water! Then I'll never be thirsty again, and I won't have to come here to get water." "Go and get your husband," Jesus told her.

"I don't have a husband," the woman replied. Jesus said, "You're right! You don't have a husband — for you have had five husbands, and you aren't even married to the man you're living with now. You certainly spoke the truth!" John 4:15-18 (NLT)

The woman had five husbands and was now living with another man. Wow! These choices might be common in the 21st century, but they certainly weren't the norm back in Jesus' day. What was this woman thinking? Was she fickle? Were her expectations and standards of a husband too high? What was it that she didn't learn from the first, second, third, fourth, and fifth marriage? Or was she clingy and riddled with insecurities which caused her men to leave her? The Scriptures don't give us the answers. All we know is that she made some poor choices and the marriage covenant was broken. Now she willingly chose to live in unrepentant sin. And guess what? She was thirsty because of it.

I feel like I know this woman, probably because I'm a lot like her. Before I became a born-again Christian I was married once before but then divorced the man because he became abusive. Being that I didn't want to live through a marriage like that again, I shacked up with my next boyfriend.

Somewhere along the lines of life you just lose hope, at least that was my case. You don't think you'll ever find Mr. Right and have your happily ever after, so you settle for second best.

The beauty of this story is that the Woman at the Well decided she was no longer going to settle. She needed Jesus, the Living Water, to quench her spiritual thirst. No husband, not even a great man of God can quench the thirst that only Jesus Christ can give you.

Lessons to Learn from the Life of the Woman at the Well....

- ♥ She realized she needed Jesus Christ as her Lord and Savior.

- ♥ Our husband is not designed to complete us; only Jesus Christ holds this position.

❧ Application ☙

Regardless of your past or present circumstances, let the Lord quench your soul in your marriage. Run to Him for nourishment, acceptance, and love.

Perhaps you've made some of the same choices that the Woman at the Well made, and you're having a hard time dealing with it, then my encouragement and exhortation to you is to run to the Redeemer. Dwell on Him and what He did on the Cross for *you*. Don't head into the Land of Condemnation because that land is not of Jesus Christ, that land is straight from the pit of hell, from Satan himself.

The Enemy wants you to remain in this land as long as possible, but if you could just turn your eyes to the Cross and meditate on the Word of God, you'll get out of this land sooner than you think!

Don't allow the past sins of your life that our precious Savior died on the cross for, have a stronghold in your marriage.

For by grace you have been saved through faith, and that not of yourselves; it is the gift of God, not of works, lest anyone should boast. Eph. 2:8,9

Lesson 15

The Discerning Wife

She was married to a rude and wicked man.

Her husband's servants even had disdain for him.

Yet this wife was a woman of good understanding.

She protected the life of her husband as well as her whole household.

So who is this wife?

She's Abigail, wife of Nabal.

Here's her story…

> The name of the man was Nabal, and the name of his wife Abigail.

And she was a woman of good understanding and beautiful appearance; but the man was harsh and evil in his doings. 1 Sam. 25:3 Now one of the young men told Abigail, Nabal's wife, saying, "Look, David sent messengers from the wilderness to greet our master; and he reviled them. "But the men were very good to us, and we were not hurt, nor did we miss anything as long as we accompanied them, when we were in the fields. "They were a wall to us both by night and day, all the time we were with them keeping the sheep. "Now therefore, know and consider what you will do, for harm is determined against our master and against all his household. For he is such a scoundrel that one cannot speak to him." Then Abigail made haste and took two hundred loaves of bread, two skins of wine, five sheep already dressed, five seahs of roasted grain, one hundred clusters of raisins, and two hundred cakes of figs, and loaded them on donkeys. And she said to her servants, "Go on before me; see, I am coming after you." But she did not tell her husband Nabal. So it was, as she rode on the donkey, that she went down under cover of the hill; and there were David and his men, coming down toward her, and she met them. Now David had said, "Surely in vain I have protected all that this fellow has in the wilderness, so that nothing was missed of all that belongs to him. And he has repaid me evil for good. 1 Sam. 25:14-21

Now when Abigail saw David, she dismounted quickly from the donkey, fell on her face before David, and bowed down to the ground. So she fell at his feet and said: "On me, my lord, on me let this iniquity be! And please let your maidservant speak in your ears, and hear the words of your maidservant. "Please, let not my lord regard this scoundrel Nabal. For as his name is, so is he: Nabal is his name, and folly is with him! But I, your maidservant, did not see the young men of my lord whom you sent. "Now therefore, my lord, as the LORD lives and as your soul lives, since the LORD has held you back from coming to bloodshed and from avenging yourself with your own hand, now then, let your enemies and those who seek harm for my lord be as Nabal. 1 Sam. 25:23-26

Regardless of the lack of Godly character that Nabal possessed, Abigail was of woman of good understanding. She used her influence to persuade David to spare her family and their servants from his wrath.

David heeded her voice and respected her. 1 Samuel 25:35

She used discernment as to when she should speak to her wicked and drunk husband and when to remain silent.

Now Abigail went to Nabal, and there he was, holding a feast in his house, like the feast of a king. And Nabal's heart was merry within him, for he was very drunk; therefore she told him nothing, little or much, until morning light. So it was, in the morning, when the wine had gone from Nabal, and his wife had told him these things, that his heart died within him, and he became like a stone. 1 Sam. 25:36,37 Then it happened, after about ten days, that the LORD struck Nabal, and he died. So when David heard that Nabal was dead, he said, "Blessed be the LORD, who has pleaded the cause of my reproach from the hand of Nabal, and has kept His servant from evil! For the LORD has returned the wickedness of Nabal on his own head." And David sent and proposed to Abigail, to take her as his wife. 1 Sam. 25:38,39

Lessons to Learn from the Life of Abigail…

- ♥ Abigail lived with a wicked, overbearing and harsh man but she kept the right perspective when disaster came upon her household. Her ultimate goal was saving the lives of her family and making sure David, the future King, did not get blood on his hands because he killed out of vengeance.

♥ Abigail didn't betray her husband in seeking to provide supplies to David; instead, she sought to save Nabal's life. She acted swiftly and with humility taking the blame for why David's men greeted Nabal and not her.

♥ Abigail followed the Lord but her husband didn't. She sought to bring peace into the household in spite of her husband's harsh ways.

❧ Application ❦

Perhaps your husband has done some foolish things in your marriage from time to time? Or maybe he's an unbeliever or not walking right with the Lord? If your faith is deeper than your man's here are 10 practical tips to help you bridge the spiritual gap in your marriage.

1. Pray to be a discerning wife in your marriage. Ask God to give you wisdom and understanding when dealing with your guy.

2. Keep growing in your relationship with the Lord. Don't lessen up your pursuit of Christ just because your husband's faith is not as strong as yours.

3. Make sure you don't condemn, criticize, or nag your man for not having the depths of faith that you have.

4. If God gave you the spiritual gift of faith, my encouragement to you would be to memorize Romans 12:3. God gave you that beautiful gift to bring Christ glory, not to make your husband feel like a worthless spiritual leader.

5. Learn to become more understanding and gracious when your husband's faith can't move a mountain.

6. Ask him how you can pray for him and then ask him if he can pray for you too. This act shows your man your softness, humility, and vulnerability. A husband is drawn to these virtues.

7. Submit to God and surrender all areas of your life to Him....even when it is oh, so difficult! Let the Holy Spirit lead your husband spiritually, rather than you having the attitude that you need to lead your man. God won't let you down. He'll protect you and He'll be by your side.

8. Ask your husband questions with a loving heart. Ask him how he wants to handle certain situations. This shows him that you value his opinions and it shows him that you desire his leadership. Plus, it also helps him to step forward and lead. This is a very small thing, but it can make a huge impact in your marriage.

9. Initiate spiritual conversations. Ask him what he thought about the message given that day at church. Find out what he got out of it, etc. and be prepared to share your thoughts on it as well. Ask him about some things in the Bible that you don't understand (even if you think he won't know the answer.) This might encourage him to open up the Bible and find the answers. This is something you can do together and then discuss your findings. All these things should be done in a non-threatening and non-judgmental way.

10. If you are married to an unbeliever....you can still do some of these things but you'll need to tailor it to fit your specific situation. Some husbands are not angry towards God and therefore they may be a little more open to what you have to share, but others can be hostile towards the Gospel message and a lot of these things you can't discuss with them. Remember, it is your conduct that may win him over, not your words.

Wives, likewise, be submissive to your own husbands, that even if some do not obey the word, they, without a word, may be won by the conduct of their wives, when they observe your chaste conduct accompanied by fear.
1 Peter 3:1,2

Lesson 16

The Wife of Sweet Perfume

She was a wife filled with wisdom.

She had a heart to please her Maker.

She wanted her life to emanate the sweet aroma of Jesus Christ.

She poured out this desire so she could help other wives live in such a way that they would bring honor and glory to the Lord.

So who is this wife?

They are the wives of Titus 2:3-5

Here's their story…

These older women must train the younger women to love their husbands and their children, to live wisely and be pure, to work in their homes, to do good, and to be submissive to their husbands. Then they will not bring shame on the word of God. Titus 2:3-5 (NLT)

Being that I didn't have a Christian upbringing, these wives taught me how to live the Christian life as a wife and mother. They laid out for me a biblical blueprint of my role as to what was pleasing to the Lord and why. I loved learning from them, however, I must say living a dedicated life to the Lord has been very difficult to emulate because it requires me to lay down my pride and bring my flesh to death on a daily basis!

The teaching of these older wives are very simple, yet so hard to live out.

Main Principle to Learn from the Titus 2 Wives

Live in such a way where your actions, attitudes and choices reflect the love, grace, peace and truth of your Maker.

How to Live Out this Principle

- Love your husband which comes before loving your children.

- Tend to your home.

- Respect and follow your man.

This all sounds impossible, doesn't it? Well it is if we try to do this in our flesh. But with God, all things are possible.

> *And walk in love, as Christ also has loved us and given Himself for us, an offering and a sacrifice to God for a sweet-smelling aroma. Eph. 5:2*

How do you walk in love? Walk in Jesus Christ. Be filled with the Holy Spirit and let the Spirit be the driving force in your life rather than your flesh.

The 'Why' Behind this Principle

If we live out this principle then our lives won't bring shame to the gospel message.

> *Give careful thought to the paths for your feet and be steadfast in all your ways. Prov. 4:26*

Lessons to Learn from the Titus 2 Wives...

- ♥ Love your man. A husband will feel most loved by you if you give him respect.

- ♥ Love your children. Care for them physically, emotionally, mentally and most importantly, spiritually. Make sure you invest in their spiritual lives as you shepherd them to live for the Savior.

- ♥ Make wise, God-honoring decisions in your life.

- ♥ Make your home a haven for your family.

---

৯৯ Application ৩৬

Every God-fearing wife is a work in progress. Be patient with your spiritual growth. Don't beat yourself up if you're not measuring up to *your* standards. Follow the convictions and leading of the Holy Spirit in your life and don't listen to the condemning lies the nasty snake speaks to you.

Is there a younger woman that you can minister to? Pray about mentoring her. When we mentor others, it brings a level of accountability into our own lives and it impacts our marriage for good. Mentoring helps us walk our talk.

Lesson 17

The Wife Who Wasn't a Doormat

Her husband was a ruler.

She was fearful of him.

She needed to stand up for what was right, even if it meant her death.

So who is this wife?

She's Queen Esther, wife to King Xerxes.

Here's her story...

> And the king loved Esther above all the women, and she obtained grace and favor in his sight more than all the virgins; so that he

set the royal crown upon her head, and made her queen instead of Vashti. Esther 2:17

"Go, gather together all the Jews who are in Susa, and fast for me. Do not eat or drink for three days, night or day. I and my maids will fast as you do. When this is done, I will go to the king, even though it is against the law. And if I perish, I perish." Esther 4:16

Esther's husband was a King; a ruler. He was used to getting his way all the time. Everyone bowed down to him, literally. And people were at his beck and call, literally. Life revolved around him and his kingdom. If you approached the King without being summoned you could be put to death. This was Esther's fear. She was going against the laws of the land and she knew she could be killed as a result of this act. But she also knew what was about to take place in the land was even worse; the annihilation of the Jews, her people, and *herself*.

Esther found grace and favor in the Kings' eyes when he chose her to be his wife. Just like you found grace and favor in your man's eyes when he placed a ring on your finger and he asked you to be his wife. But in some marriages today, a husband could act like a ruler instead of loving his wife like Christ loved the Church.

Now I personally don't really identify with Esther because I'm not one to shy away from confrontation no matter who it is. I'd rather be dead than be trampled on like a doormat. It's just the way I'm wired. However, I know this is not the case for all wives. Some women are non-confrontational and when you put them in a marital relationship with a natural leader/aggressive man then it can be quite easy for the wife to start to feel unheard or unloved by her man.

I have a friend who would most likely identify with Esther. She's wired as a peacekeeper and one who dislikes conflict. For a woman who avoids confrontation like the plague, it takes her a lot of strength to speak up. And for a woman who is assertive, like me, it takes me a lot of strength to keep my mouth shut. We both use strength in our marriages but in different ways. Now mind you, the strength comes from the power of the Holy Spirit, not from us.

I've spent many years with my peacekeeper friend as I've mentored her. Over the years she's had a hard time bringing up concerns and issues with her man. On numerous occasions it was difficult for her to share her heart with her husband because it generally led to an argument and nothing ever got resolved.

For a non-confrontational woman, this was like death for her. However, she wanted to be heard and she didn't want bitterness growing in her heart towards her husband. Her man had to learn to love her and the only way he could do that was for her to let him know how she was feeling. After all, men are not mind readers.

Since this man wanted to please the Lord, he was open to hearing his wife's appeals. With the Holy Spirit piercing his heart, lots of determination and many apologies later, their marriage is now flourishing. Was it easy for my friend? No. But she doesn't regret speaking up and sharing her heart with her man.

Now back to Esther...

Esther used prayer and fasting to give her the boldness needed to go before the King, as well as seeking God's favor so she wouldn't be killed. After she invited the King to her banquet, she used discernment as to when it was the best time to have the discussion with him about her people. The King was very receptive to her pleas because she came to him in a humble and gracious fashion. We know how Esther's story ends. The King said to ask up to half his kingdom, meaning whatever you ask, I'll give it to you. I'm sure with a statement like that Esther felt very loved and cherished by her guy. The neat thing about this story is through prayer, fasting and sharing her heart with her man, she helped her husband to love her and meet her needs, thus creating a deeper level of *one flesh* in their marriage. She used her influence for good and not evil.

Now here's something for you to think about if you find yourself married to a man that acts like a ruler. Esther had nothing to lose if she approached the King. Either way she would have been set to die.

If she didn't approach him, she was certain to die based on the decree that went out in the land. If she did approach him, according to the Law, a person could be put to death unless the King found favor with them. So Esther took a risk.

Now my friend, you have two choices...

1) You can *not* rock your martial boat and live with bitterness growing in your heart. (Your marriage will just grow worse as a result of this. I'm not an advocate of this path, by the way.)

2) Or you can step out in faith and talk with your man. But let me give you a warning about this path....your marriage will get worse before it'll get better. Now why do I say this? Because you'll have to work through a bunch of issues, lay down your pride and keep communicating until your problems are resolved. This is no easy task, by the way.

Here's a simple premise to give you an idea of what I'm talking about....Imagine you haven't cleaned your home in years. Would you be a little overwhelmed at the task at hand? Yeah, I'd say slightly! There's filth and dust everywhere you turn. Well, what happens when you start cleaning something that's dusty? The dust gets kicked up and it's all over the place, isn't it? It's the exact same deal when you've lived years in a marriage where you've just swept everything under the rug so you could keep the peace.

Note to a newlywed wife: don't do this! Learn to resolve your issues as soon as possible so you can maintain the love and respect your marriage was founded upon.

Okay, girlfriend, start cleaning house, but be prepared for the Enemy to show up with more trash than you already realized because he doesn't want your marriage to get better.

Lessons to Learn from the Life of Esther...

- ♥ Have the courage to share your heart with your husband even if it leads to conflict. Make sure when you speak to your man you do it in a respectful and loving way. If you can't imagine what this looks like, picture yourself talking with Jesus as you share your heart with Him.

- ♥ Win over your husband's heart and his trust so you can be an influence in his life. Your man's heart should soften towards you as a result of your loyalty and physical affection towards him. Note I said *should*. Not all husbands are willing to submit to God's Word or they don't know how. Your conduct of softness and humility will make a much greater impact on your man rather than a contentious, bitter spirit.

❧ Application ❦

Minister to your man and do so according to his love language. Pour into him without expecting anything in return. You're connecting with him when you do this. And when a wife connects with her husband, he *generally* listens to her.

- If his love language is quality time, then plan something that he enjoys doing and do it with him.

- If it's words of praise and affirmation, praise that man up and down and do it in front of others when he's in earshot.

- If he feels loved when you serve him, then make him his favorite dinner and dessert. Go all out for him. Serve it up on a tray and let him watch TV while he eats it.

- If he loves receiving gifts, study him and find out what are some things he'd like to have. Be intentional about purchasing it for him.

- If it's physical touch, give him a back rub, let your hands linger on him, give him a tight embrace. Initiate physical intimacy.

Lesson 18

The Wife Who Didn't Nag

Her spirit was disturbed.

She knew something wasn't right.

She shared her thoughts and concerns with her man but he didn't heed her warning.

This wife didn't nag, but she could have.

So who is she?

She's Pontius Pilate's wife.

Definition of nagging:
1. To annoy by constant scolding, complaining, or urging.
2. To torment persistently, as with anxiety or pain.

If you happen to have a 2 yr. old child then you probably know what nagging looks like...
"Mommy, can I have this?"

"Can I Mommy?"

"Can I?"

"When can I have it, Mommy?"

Nagging can wear on any mother's nerves.

Now apply this same premise to your marriage when you asked your man to do something. How many times did you ask him? More than once?

Well, Pontius Pilate's wife was not a known nag. She mentioned something to her husband just once. While Pilate was sitting on the judgment seat determining whether or not he should release Jesus Christ, his wife sent him this message:

> "Don't have anything to do with that innocent man, for I have suffered a great deal today in a dream because of him." Matthew 27:19

Here's something you'll find interesting...

Mrs. P was not a follower of Jesus; however, she knew something wasn't right about crucifying Jesus. Her spirit stirred within her.

This wife was more discerning than her husband, yet she was still respectful towards her man.

There's a danger in nagging your husband. When you nag him you'll push him away from you rather than draw him closer. And when you've pushed your man away it'll be harder for you to influence him.

Lessons to Learn from the Life of Pontius Pilate's Wife...

- ♥ She told her husband what was on her heart and then she let it go. She didn't bring it up again. If he didn't heed what she said or asked, the consequences were on him.

- ♥ Her spiritual understanding was deeper than her husband's; however, she didn't parent or nag her man. So if you're married to a man that's an unbeliever or barely believing, just because you're more spiritually mature than he is, you still don't want to nag him. Nagging is annoying. Remember the 2 yr. old analogy? If you're like a constant dripping faucet, your husband will tune you out and your relationship will suffer as a result of this.

❧ Application ❧

Let things go. Don't ask your husband more than once to do something that's eating at you. If you've asked him to take out the trash and he hasn't, then let it spill onto the floor. If you're a neat-freak, control-freak or a perfectionist, I know this will be hard for you. And why do I know this, because I'm in recovery in all those areas too!

Lesson 19

The Enticing Wife

She's insecure with her outer appearance. (I love her already!)

She let's her husband sexually delight in her.

She sexually delights in him.

But then she rejects him.

So who is this wife?

She's the Shulamite woman, also known as Solomon's wife.

Here's her story...

> Don't stare at me because I am dark— the sun has darkened my skin.

My brothers were angry with me; they forced me to care for their vineyards, so I couldn't care for myself—my own vineyard. Song of Solomon 1:6 (NLT)

She has insecurities and she's embarrassed with her body. *Can you relate?* But she sexually desires her man and she can't get enough of him.

Kiss me and kiss me again, for your love is sweeter than wine. Song of Solomon 1:2

The Hebrew noun for love in this verse means sexual love. Awe, remember those days, my friend? The days when you couldn't get enough of your man? And your heart beat so fast for him?

Solomon sexually desires her and he's drawn in and intoxicated by his bride.

You have captured my heart, my treasure, my bride. You hold it hostage with one glance of your eyes, with a single jewel of your necklace. Your love delights me, my treasure, my bride. Your love is better than wine, your perfume more fragrant than spices. Your lips are as sweet as nectar, my bride. Honey and milk are under your tongue. Your clothes are scented like the cedars of Lebanon. Song of Solomon 4:9-11

But the Shulamite woman denies her man...

She's already gone to bed. She doesn't want to get up and let him in because she'll get her feet dirty. This just cracked me up when I read it. In essence, she's telling her man she's tired.

> I slept, but my heart was awake, when I heard my lover knocking and calling: "Open to me, my treasure, my darling, my dove, my perfect one. My head is drenched with dew, my hair with the dampness of the night." But I responded, "I have taken off my robe. Should I get dressed again? I have washed my feet. Should I get them soiled?" My lover tried to unlatch the door, and my heart thrilled within me. I jumped up to open the door for my love, and my hands dripped with perfume. My fingers dripped with lovely myrrh as I pulled back the bolt. I opened to my lover, but he was gone! My heart sank. Song of Solomon 5:2-6

She realizes she messed up when she turned him away. But then she goes after him to try to restore their relationship.

> I searched for him but could not find him anywhere. I called to him, but there was no reply. Song of Solomon 5:6

Lessons to Learn from Solomon's Wife...

♥ In spite of your insecurities, listen to your husband when he tells you you're beautiful. (Song of Solomon 6:4)

♥ If you deny your man of sexual intimacy, then work on restoring it in your relationship. Make sure you apologize and don't head down that path again. It's better that you're honest with him as to why you don't want to have sex than to keep denying him for no good reason.

♥ Make yourself visually beautiful for your man because men are visual.

♥ Sexually delight in your husband and let him fully delight in you. When you're fully participating and enjoying the act of marriage, guess what? You're man is even more into you.

♥ Here's a line you'll never want to use in your marriage....*I'm sorry honey, but not tonight because I'll get my feet dirty!* To us that sounds absurd because we have showers in our homes but that wasn't the case for Solomon's wife. People back then wore sandals and walked around on dirt so they had dirty feet all the time. Remember how Jesus washed the disciples' feet? That was the norm for the times. Anyways, the reason I pointed this out was because the Shulamite woman was just like you and me; tired and busy. They had dirty feet; we get tired or have headaches. (Oh, and let's not forget she was insecure too!) Same issues just different lifestyles.

℘ Application ℘

- Don't deny your man because it'll bring damage to your marriage, furthermore, you'll run the risk of opening your relationship up to being attacked by the Enemy. God designed sex in marriage to be a fabulous thing. It strengthens your loyalty to each other and it connects you physically, emotionally, and spiritually.

- Dress yourself in a way that you know your husband would like, kind of like you did when you were newly married. Is there a certain outfit he likes you in? Does he like your hair worn a certain way? A particular perfume he enjoys? Put forth some effort to show him how much you desire him. Throw the sweatpants and slippers in the closet, girlfriend, and put on something sexy. It's okay. You can do it. You're married!

- If you're not very intimate with your man, why is that? What has changed in your marriage that you don't want to have sex with him? Is it because additional responsibilities have been added to your plate?

- Does he expect too much from you? See if you can lessen some of your commitments so you'll have more energy for him (and you!)

- Something you can do is plan your times of intimacy so you're refreshed and looking forward to when the two of you will be together. I think this plan is imperative when you're in the midst of raising a family and you're exhausted. Hey, we plan play-dates for the kiddos, doctor's appts., sporting events, church, etc. Why not plan for sex?

- Another benefit for a wife to plan for physical intimacy is because sex is a huge mental thing for women. When you're looking forward to being intimate with your husband that day, you're in essence putting yourself in the mood, which will help you to desire your man more. This little thing will increase your sex-drive if yours happens to be non-existent..

Here's something you might find interesting about Solomon...

Although he was deeply in love with his wife, he still had business to attend to; he had a kingdom to run. He couldn't be with his woman all the time nor could he always focus on her. It was the same premise with his wife. She had other responsibilities as well. (Solomon 6:1-3)

It's easy for a wife to feel neglected once the honeymoon period is over, but don't allow your mind to go there. The two of you are just building your lives together. However, don't neglect your intimacy. Be intentional about having it. That's why you married your man in the first place, right? So you could have sex with him? That's why I married my man, otherwise we'd just be good friends!

Liz & Kenny!

Lesson 20

The Radical Wife

I love the type of marriage this wife had with her husband. I view their relationship as one of the most successful marriages in the Bible and I deem it to be the type of marriage a Christian couple should try to emulate.

This wife served side by side with her husband in ministry.

Her life was not about what she could get out of her marriage, but what her marriage could give to the Lord.

So who is this wife?

She's Priscilla, wife of Aquila.

Here's her story…

Priscilla and Aquila were always mentioned together in the Scriptures. You didn't read about the one without the other. I see these two as truly one flesh as they've put their own desires aside so the can further advance the Kingdom of God. This type of marriage displays self-control and contentment at it's finest.

This couple served side by side with the Apostle Paul as they learned from him and then went on to minister to others. Priscilla and Aquila even held church in their own home.

> The churches of Asia greet you. Aquila and Priscilla greet you heartily in the Lord, with the church that is in their house. 1 Cor. 16:19

They further instructed others in sound doctrine.

> So he began to speak boldly in the synagogue. When Aquila and Priscilla heard him, they took him aside and explained to him the way of God more accurately. Acts 18:26

And they put their own lives on the line to help the Apostle Paul to further advance the kingdom of God.

> Greet Priscilla and Aquila, my fellow workers in Christ Jesus, who risked their own necks for my life, to whom not only I give thanks, but also all the churches of the Gentiles. Romans 16:3,4

Priscilla was heavenly minded.

She had a radical faith about her. Her goal in life was to please the Lord as she went about ministering to others. Often times we come into marriage expecting our union to make us happy, when our goal, as Christians, should really be to make us holy as we come together as husband and wife to further advance the Gospel. Unfortunately, this is not the case for many Christian marriages. Often times we get caught up with our own desires or we're too consumed with self and the building of our kingdoms that we can't see clearly enough to serve the Lord. We build an altar of petty disagreements or pity parties instead of seeking to please the Lord with our marriage. This was something I had to learn over the course of my marriage.

But Priscilla learned that life was not about her, it was about the Lord and lifting Him up for all to see. This radical pursuit of hers definitely impacted her marriage because no self-centered and prideful wife would be able to do ministry with her husband on a regular basis and still see spiritual fruit from it. Priscilla was a mature Believer who brought her flesh under control and her life reflected it.

We are here for the Lord.

> For we are His workmanship, created in Christ Jesus for good works, which God prepared beforehand that we should walk in them. Epehsians 2:10

Lessons to Learn from the Life of Priscilla...

♥ Priscilla's life was about her Father's business. She sought to serve others in the name of the Lord but she had to die to her flesh, *daily*, in order to continually pour out her life for Christ.

✌ Application ⚘

When your marriage has harmony (not perfection) and your children are being guided and trained (but they're not perfect), then venture on out of your comfort zone and be the salt and light as a married couple as you serve the Lord.

"And behold, I am coming quickly, and My reward is with Me, to give to every one according to his work. Rev. 22:12

Lesson 21

The Respectful Wife

This wife challenges me to the core.

When I think about all that she endured I can't help but shed a few tears because of her heartache and pain.

She was the talk of the town. Her good name was being smeared.

Her man didn't initially want to marry her because of rumors, lies, and misunderstandings. I would imagine that response must have broken her heart.

But he took her as his wife because the Lord told him to do so.

Although her marriage started off a little rocky and rather unique, she followed her man, nonetheless.

Regardless of her circumstances, she had a surrendered spirit; seeking to please her Father above all others.

This dear wife based her life on ~~faith~~, not ~~logic~~.

So who is this wife?

She's Mary, the wife of Joseph.

Mary and Joseph are engaged to be married when Mary gets greeted by an angel telling her she will conceive a Child; the Messiah. I can't even imagine what initially went through Mary's mind when this all took place. Fear? What will the neighbors think? How am I going to explain this to Joseph and my parents? Will they even believe me? Perhaps that's why she took off to her cousin Elisabeth's house? She's now a public disgrace because she's pregnant outside of wedlock.

> This is how the birth of Jesus Christ came about: His mother Mary was pledged to be married to Joseph, but before they came together, she was found to be with child through the Holy Spirit. Because Joseph her husband was a righteous man and did not want to expose her to public disgrace, he had in mind to divorce her quietly. But after he had considered this, an angel of the Lord appeared to him in a dream and said, "Joseph son of David, do not be afraid to take Mary home as your wife, because what is conceived

in her is from the Holy Spirit. Matthew 1:18-20

Respectful Act #1

Mary marries Joseph even though earlier he was going to privately divorce her.

> So all went to be registered, everyone to his own city. Joseph also went up from Galilee, out of the city of Nazareth, into Judea, to the city of David, which is called Bethlehem, because he was of the house and lineage of David, to be registered with Mary, his betrothed wife, who was with child.
> Luke 2:3-5

Respectful Act #2

Mary followed Joseph to Bethlehem to be counted for the census.

Let's take a look at this for a second, shall we? From Nazareth to Bethlehem it's 80 miles. If you traveled on foot for 20 miles a day, you'd reach Bethlehem in 4 days. However, Mary was ready to deliver the Baby at any time.

Imagine journeying across rugged terrain when you're fully pregnant riding a donkey, with your first child, nonetheless. Not to mention the fact that the man you're travelling with initially wanted to divorce you.

Oh, yeah, let's just add to this mix that you're carrying the Savior of the World! I don't know about you, but I would have lost it! Hmm, perhaps that's one of the many reasons why God chose Mary to carry, deliver, and raise up Jesus, rather then choosing me to do it. And let's not forget that Mary had free will. She had a choice, she didn't have to follow Joseph, but she respected him and followed him in the midst of these circumstances. She was one obedient woman.

> Now when they had departed, behold, an angel of the Lord appeared to Joseph in a dream, saying, "Arise, take the young Child and His mother, flee to Egypt, and stay there until I bring you word; for Herod will seek the young Child to destroy Him." When he arose, he took the young Child and His mother by night and departed for Egypt. Matthew 2:13,14

Respectful Act #3

Mary followed Joseph as he took her and the Child to Egypt.

Lessons to Learn from the Life of Mary...

- ♥ She submitted to the Lord in her difficult circumstances, which in turn, caused her to have a respectful heart towards her husband.

- ♥ While I realize God chose Mary to be the mother of Jesus, she was still a human being.

She still had feelings and I'm sure at times she was fearful of their situation. She could have bickered and argued with Joseph, or she could've just followed his lead and prayed for the Lord to guide and protect them. I think Mary chose the latter of the two based on her attitude when the Lord told her He's chosen her to carry His son. I believe Mary was filled with wisdom and she was content in following the Lord's plan for her life even if she couldn't see where it was going to lead her. That woman respected her man because that, my friend, is God's plan for a Godly wife!

♥ As I look at their marital relationship, Mary learned to rely on Joseph as they lived through their trials and afflictions. She was okay in not trying to prove herself to her man. She wasn't trying to be some kind of superwoman. She rested in not only the Lord's strength, but Joseph's as well.

♥ She willingly accepted his protection and his leadership. She didn't fight him to be in that headship position.

♥ She followed and respected him.

♥ Mary's marriage was not about her. Her goal was to bring glory to the Lord through her surrendered heart and devotion to her Father.

💜 When you're faced with the struggles of this life, lean into your man, don't pull away from him or blame him for your trials. Remember that you can't see God's plan for your life but you can read His Word and know how to walk in His ways.

💜 Respecting your man may seem impossible for you but it isn't for God! This is the verse the angel, Gabriel said to Mary when she said to him how will it be possible for me to conceive since I am a virgin?

For nothing is impossible with God." Luke 1:37

✎ Application ✎

Give your man respect. Below are a few ideas to help you get started in this lifelong journey,

6 Ways to Show Your Husband Respect

- Follow his lead.
- Don't fight his headship position.
- Give him eye contact when he's speaking to you.
- Speak highly of him in front of others.
- Be a joyful and content wife.
- Serve him. A simple thing I do in my home is I serve my husband his meal before I serve my children. This shows my man respect and at the same time it teaches my boys what a respectful wife looks like.

Now you may think that some of the things on this list are impossible to do. Well, perhaps they are but I want to remind you of Mary's response when she received the news from the angel that she was going to conceive...

"I am the Lord's servant," Mary answered. "May it be to me as you have said." Luke 1:38

What a great and humble attitude to have in life.

If you've lost respect for your husband, here are 4 ways to recapture it.

1. Be mindful of your own sins, shortcomings, and failures.

2. Be forgiving and gracious towards him.

3. Extend him your compassion and mercy.

4. Find at least 5 things you respect about him and dwell on those things. Over time, you'll come to respect him more. Be patient with this process.

These tips can't be done in your own strength, you need to lean on the Lord and allow the Holy Spirit to move in your heart and give you the strength from His power.

Lesson 22

The Submissive Wife

I love this wife.

She was bold and radical.

She was strong and willing to go against family, friends, customs and traditions.

Yet, she submitted to her husband. *What? She submitted to her man? Did she lose her mind? Why would any woman willingly submit to their husband? Hmmm, perhaps she knew something about submission that others didn't?*

So who is this wife?

She's Elizabeth, the wife of Zacharias.

In my book, she is one Godly woman to emulate.

Let's get a few things straight, first. A submissive wife does not mean a silent wife. It does not mean you don't have an opinion of your own and you can't think for yourself. And a submissive wife doesn't mean you're a weak-minded woman either. That's quite the contrary, my friend. A submissive wife is a wife filled with wisdom and self-control. And where does wisdom come from? Wisdom comes from the Lord. Period. It doesn't come from how many books you've read, how many degrees you have, or what advice you've heard from Oprah or Dr. Phil.

The fear of the Lord is the beginning of wisdom.
Proverbs 9:10

Elizabeth had wisdom. She was known as a righteous woman before God, walking in all the commands and ordinances. She was faithful to God. (Luke 1:6)

But first, what's the big deal about submission anyways?

Why do we keep hearing this message? Well, here are a few reasons:

•   It's not in our nature to submit. Our spirit is always at war with our fleshly tendencies, so being reminded of this message is a good thing. Kind of like you telling your child to grab a coat because it's going to be cold outside. Your child is not thinking about the weather, or he thinks he won't need a jacket, but you know he will. You know he'll be cold so you want to protect him.

It's the same thing when wives are telling other wives to submit to their own husbands. We know a good thing when we see it.

• God tells us to submit. That was reason enough for me when I read the verse many years ago. You see, I ran my life into the gutter before I came to Christ and when I acknowledged my need for a Savior, I surrendered my life to Him. I gave Him the reins, or the steering wheel of my life. I wanted Him to be the driver. I wanted to follow His lead because I believed He knew what was best for me and He wouldn't steer me wrong.

However, I must say when I first read about the whole submission thing I totally thought God screwed up! When the Lord said the husband is the head of the home I was rather disgusted with that verse. Now mind you, I was a take charge kind of woman. So that verse really bothered me. Hence that was the main reason why I was not in a hurry to marry; I wasn't looking to submit to some man anytime soon. But what I couldn't reconcile in my mind was if the man was to be the leader of the home, then why did God give me such a strong personality? I really thought God should have made me the male; the leader. I so seriously thought this! My personality was more suited to be in charge. I wasn't a helper, (scoff), to anyone! How on earth was I going to follow someone?

I was, and still am, an outspoken, strong-willed, highly opinionated, type-A personality.

I'm a driver; well I was until I became chronically ill for all those years, (that'll cause you to end up in the back seat real quick!) God has a way of tempering us, doesn't He?

When I came to Christ, I knew it was going to take an act of God for this woman to have a gentle and quite spirit (1 Peter 3:4). By the way, God does do miracles! So I share all of this to tell you where I've come from and to show you how God has transformed me. He'll transform you as well if you want Him to.

Now back to Elisabeth.

Remember the story of when her hubby, Zacharias, the High Priest went into the Temple to burn incense as was customary back in the day? Well, the angel, Gabriel showed up and told Zach that his woman, who was well past the age of childbearing, was indeed going to be pregnant. Of course, like any normal human being, Zacharias couldn't possibly believe the angel. Goodness, could you blame him? Well, that didn't make Gabriel too happy so he told Zacharias that the Lord is going to close up his mouth until the babe was born.

> But Gabriel left Zacharias with an implicit order. The child to be born will be the prophet of the Highest (Luke 1:76) and his name is to be called John. (Luke 1:13)

Elisabeth delivers a baby in her old age. They go to circumcise him on the 8th day as was the custom, and they name the baby.

> When the baby was eight days old, they all came for the circumcision ceremony. They wanted to name him Zacharias, after his father. But Elizabeth said, "No! His name is John!" "What?" they exclaimed. "There is no one in all your family by that name." So they used gestures to ask the baby's father what he wanted to name him. He motioned for a writing tablet, and to everyone's surprise he wrote, "His name is John." Instantly Zacharias could speak again, and he began praising God. Luke 1:59-64 (NLT)

I wish I were standing in the room when this all came down. I could see Elizabeth telling everyone that they need to back up! Nothing and no one is going to keep her from obeying her God and her man. I love how adamant she was when she spoke to her family. And the nerve they had to discount what she had to say as they used gestures to speak with Zacharias. Perhaps the idea of throwing them out of her house crossed her mind at that point? I know it would've crossed my mind. The gal had tenacity and she was going to follow the Lord's command at all costs.

Lessons to Learn from the Life of Elizabeth...

- ❤ She didn't allow her relatives and friends to influence her to go against her Lord and her husband. She was not easily swayed.

- ❤ She was one strong-minded woman not afraid to stand up for what was right, regardless of popular opinions, customs, and traditions.

- ❤ She submitted to the Lord and she submitted to her husband even when her man couldn't speak to her for nine months. There's some one flesh unity going on in that marriage.

- ❤ She put her faith and trust in the Lord in spite of what others were saying.

I believe that God blessed Elizabeth's faithfulness and obedience tremendously. The Lord chose her to carry and raise up a son, John the Baptist. Jesus, the Savior of the World, deemed him as being the greatest prophet. That's some pretty high accolades, don't you think?

"Assuredly, I say to you, among those born of women there has not risen one greater than John the Baptist." Matthew 11:11

❧ Application ❧

- When you choose to submit to your husband, you're ultimately submitting to the Lord. However, make sure you don't submit to your man's sin.

142

- Follow your husband's leadership. This shows your husband that you believe in him and this happens to make him feel respected.

Lesson 23

The Wife Who Feared the Lord

I have a love/hate relationship with this wife.

She is a wife I look up to and one I try to emulate, but she puts me to shame.

She's dedicated to her husband and children.

She's hard-working.

She's filled with graciousness, compassion, and wisdom.

She seeks to make her home comfortable for her family.

And she ministers to others.

But what stands out to me the most about this wife is not what she *did* or what she *said*, but *Who* she pursued...

She pursued the Lord.

So who is this wife?

If you've been walking with the Lord for any length of time now, then you're probably very familiar with the Proverbs 31 Woman. Generally speaking, when we learn about her we delve into all the things she does or says, but I'm not going to do that. Nope. I'm going to get to the bottom of this woman as I uncover 'why' she does what she does. We're going to see what makes this wife tick and why she arises while it's still night!

Here's her story...

> A wife of noble character who can find? She is worth far more than rubies. Her husband has full confidence in her and lacks nothing of value. She brings him good, not harm, all the days of her life. She selects wool and flax and works with eager hands. She is like the merchant ships, bringing her food from afar. She gets up while it is still dark; she provides food for her family and portions for her servant girls. She considers a field and buys it; out of her earnings she plants a vineyard. She sets about her work vigorously; her arms are strong for her tasks.

She sees that her trading is profitable, and her lamp does not go out at night. In her hand she holds the distaff and grasps the spindle with her fingers. She opens her arms to the poor and extends her hands to the needy. When it snows, she has no fear for her household; for all of them are clothed in scarlet. She makes coverings for her bed; she is clothed in fine linen and purple. Her husband is respected at the city gate, where he takes his seat among the elders of the land. She makes linen garments and sells them, and supplies the merchants with sashes. She is clothed with strength and dignity; she can laugh at the days to come. She speaks with wisdom, and faithful instruction is on her tongue. She watches over the affairs of her household and does not eat the bread of idleness. Her children arise and call her blessed; her husband also, and he praises her: "Many women do noble things, but you surpass them all." Charm is deceptive, and beauty is fleeting; but a woman who fears the LORD is to be praised. Give her the reward she has earned, and let her works bring her praise at the city gate. Proverbs 31:10-31

This wife was my very first mentor. I purposed my life in trying to become like her only to fail miserably. As a new Believer and a new bride many years ago, I passionately pursued her way of life, but there was a problem...I was physically incapable of doing so. My limitations had nothing to do with lack of discipline or lack of understanding of the Word.

No, that wasn't it. My deal was I couldn't fulfill what was laid out before me in the Scriptures because I was sick, and I don't mean for just one day, either. My illnesses went on for a decade and it started at the onset of motherhood. I became so ill that I couldn't even do the basic things like feed my children lunch on a regular basis. As a wife and mother I felt like a failure for so many years and I often wondered why the Lord would take me through so many health trials when all I wanted to do was serve Him.

In my mind, I equated doing things for the Lord to being a Godly woman and wife. Well now I can say I know why the Lord took me through those 10 long years. One of the reasons is so I can write this part of the book. He's given me some insight into this passage as a result of my trials. So I'm going to share with you what He shared with me.

We often miss the point of this passage of Scripture when all we see is this Godly wife's to do list. But hidden right at the very bottom of the passage is this:

"Many women do noble things......"

Yes, giving honor and respect to our husband is a noble thing and so is taking care of our children, our homes, ministering to others, etc. They're noble pursuits, are they not?

"But you surpass them all because you fear the LORD."

The noble things didn't make this wife Godly.

What made her Godly was she feared the Lord,
not her to-do list.

Sometimes as Christian women will feel like we need to be Superwoman when we read this passage in Proverbs, but that is the furthest thing from the Truth.

Think about some of these questions....

- Are we less Godly if we can't do all the things listed above in this passage?
- Are we spiritually lacking if we can't manage everything on the list?
- Have we fallen short because our home is not always (or ever) in tip-top condition?
- What if we're not making sashes of fine linen or even sewing buttons on clothes, does this mean we are less Christ-like than another woman who does these things?

Friend, we have been listening to that dirty-rotten snake, again. Satan is speaking lies into our hearts and minds all the time. God looks at your heart, (1 Sam. 16:7) not how much you've accomplished in a day.

While our intentions are good in wanting to emulate the
Proverbs 31 wife, we need to make sure we're more
intentional about pursuing the heart of God.

The story of Mary and Martha comes to mind when I think of this concept. Remember these two sisters? Martha's busy serving and she's bent out of shape that Mary is sitting at Jesus' feet learning from Him. Martha barks out an order to Jesus and tells Him to tell Mary to get up and help her. Jesus' response, "Martha, Martha, you are troubled about many things but Mary has chosen the better part.

Sitting at Jesus' feet is the better part, my friend. Learning from Him and being filled with His presence is the key to the heart of the Proverbs 31 wife; not how well she could sew on a button or make a linen garment. Sometimes we get the order all wrong with the Proverbs 31 wife. It's the heart that matters, not what the hands do. Our hands will naturally follow the motives of our heart.

And out of the abundance of your heart, the mouth speaks.
Luke 6:45

When your heart is filled with the love of Christ, you'll look at your man with Christ-like eyes; eyes filled with graciousness, love, patience, and mercy. You know, all those things you once had for him back in the day!

If you draw closer to Jesus, you won't be able to help yourself in giving honor and respect to your man, because that's what God wants you to do. And the more you give your man honor and respect, the more he'll trust in you and the better your marriage will be.

Again, you are a wife of influence, but you need the influence of your Savior to be a Godly wife.

The Proverb's 31 Wife is wrapped up in pleasing the Lord before pleasing others. I know when I neglect spending time with the Lord it's easier for me to go through life in my own strength rather than the strength of the Holy Spirit. As wives, we need the Holy Spirit to help us in our marriage and our family life

Lessons to Learn from the Life of the Proverb's 31 Wife...

- ♥ She had a reverent fear of her Maker.

- ♥ Her life pursuit was to please the Lord, not man.

- ♥ She willingly submitted and surrendered her life to Him.

- ♥ Her heart for the Lord led her to serve others with a willing and joyful spirit.

✎ Application ✎

Be committed about staying in the Word on a daily basis. Watch and see how this one thing will change your attitude towards your husband.

The only way to be a wife after God's own heart is if you get to know God's heart.

Lesson 24

The Transformed Wife

She had a lot of brokenness.

But instead of choosing bitterness, she chose to become better. And she did so when she walked by faith.

The Lord redeemed her.

And through His mighty hand, she became joyful and transformed.

So who is this wife?

She's Sarah, wife to Abraham.

Here's her story...
> Then God said to Abraham, "Regarding Sarai, your wife — her name will no longer be Sarai.

From now on her name will be Sarah. Genesis 17:15

For in this manner, in former times, the holy women who trusted in God also adorned themselves, being submissive to their own husbands, as Sarah obeyed Abraham, calling him lord, whose daughters you are if you do good and are not afraid with any terror. 1 Peter 3:5,6

Sarah's come a long way in her faith, has she not? You remember this wife, right? She's Sarai, the wife who told her husband to sleep with another woman so could have a baby. Then Sarai complained to Abraham about Hagar's mistreatment towards her and she said it was all his fault! Sarai's ways were self-centered and controlling and her conduct was utterly ridiculous.   But now here she is receiving praises for her faith in Christ and her submissive spirit. Go figure! Can you even imagine how she went from *The Contentious Wife* to *The Transformed Wife?*

How did it all happen? What happened to Sarai that she became Sarah? She became broken. A broken spirit can either leave you bitter or better. Sarah chose to run towards the Lord in her pain, rather than away from Him. Regardless of all the half-cocked decisions she made, there was one that made a huge difference in her life and it was this one....

In her brokenness, she submitted to the will of her Father.

God gave Sarah a new name because He had a new relationship with her. Friend, you and I are just like Sarah; we're being transformed.

But transformation hurts!

If you ever delivered a child then you know what I'm talking about. Before the baby is delivered, you walked into the hospital as a woman who was pregnant. When you walked out, you weren't. A transformation took place in the delivery room and it was no picnic! Going from pregnant to a new mother was quite the painful process.

Let me give you another example. Exercising. Ugh! When you first start working out, it's rather difficult and painful, is it not? Your muscles ache and sometimes you can barely walk because your muscles are so fatigued and overworked. As you continue this process, growth starts to take place and you get stronger. Over time, your body has changed; it's been transformed. Was it an easy process? Hardly.

It's the same premise in our spiritual lives. God takes us through times of brokenness so He can strengthen us and grow us in our faith. As we hold fast to the promises of God, in time, we become transformed. Or we can just check out on the whole walking with Christ thing because it's just too difficult.

Let me just say right now, that's not a good move, girlfriend. You may think your life is hard following Christ, I can tell you from first hand experience it would be way worse without Him.

Or how about making this choice? Continue walking with Christ but do so in a lukewarm fashion. Another bad move. You're living *between* bitter and better. There is no joy or peace in that land, just fear and discontentment.

A Transformed Wife is a Wife of Faith.

Now faith is the substance of things hoped for,
the evidence of things not seen.
Hebrews 11:1

In our marriages, we should be walking according to the Scriptures, not according to our feelings or what the world says to do. Is this easy? No way. We have to die to our flesh, daily. We have to walk in the Spirit, not our flesh. We have to be intentional about pursing Christ and not our own selfish desires. And when you do these things day after day, week after week, month after month, and year after year, guess what? We become transformed wives. We are no longer Sarai's, but Sarah's; we're wives of faith! We are wives obedient to the Scriptures because we believe in God's promises. We believe that God truly does know what He's talking about!

The Road of Transformation

On this road we become *The Wife of Sweet Perfume* as we are guided into the Truth. Here we learn the reason *why* we should love our husband, children and keep the home; it's so the Word of God is not misaligned.

On this road we become *The Submissive Wife* because we're submitting to our LORD, who tells us to submit to our lord (husband) as Sarah called her man.

On this road we become *The Respectful Wife* as we follow our husband.

On this road we become *The Wife Who Wasn't a Doormat* when we speak to our man without any fear or terror of him. (1 Peter 3:6)

On this road we become *The Enticing Wife* as we sexually delight in our husband, drawing closer to him, physically, emotionally, and spiritually.

On this road we become *The Wife Who Feared the Lord* because we've learned where true wisdom comes from. Because of the wisdom He has given to us, we joyfully serve others out of our devotion to the Lord.

On this road we become *The Radical Wife* where our marriage is not about us, but rather about the Lord and we're serving Him together in ministry.

The road of transformation is hard, but it's right in God's eyes. You may want to argue this path but let me give you a word of caution....

"What sorrow awaits those who argue with their Creator.
Isaiah 45:9

Now let's reconcile our personalities on this road, shall we?

For the assertive personalities like Sarah, God made you this way for a reason. He gave you boldness for a purpose. So instead of using your personality for evil, use it for good. The last thing my personality would scream is 'submissive', yet, I've recognized that God does indeed know what He's doing when He told wives to submit to their husbands. What I've learned to do (and still learning) is to use my controlling nature to control myself rather than others. I don't always succeed in this, by the way! But I'm intentional about this pursuit because my marital relationship is more important than my need to control.

For the non-confrontational, peacemaker personality, use your peacemaking qualities to speak your heart to your husband. When you're doing this you're creating a peaceful marriage. But realize there's a big difference between keeping the peace and making things peaceful. God gave you a beautiful sweet spirit that soothes and comforts others. You're personality is needed for the advancement of the Kingdom of God.

Discern the difference between who God made you to be and the sin that seeps out of you.

You were made by God and for God, my friend. Let your personality shine for Him but try to keep your sin under control. He's the one who grows you as He pierces your heart. And with a willing and surrendered spirit, He's the One who'll transform you.

"Behold, I make all things new." Rev. 21:5

Lessons to Learn from the Life of Sarah...

💜 Realize there's a purpose for the pain that you're going through.

💜 Surrender your life to God because it's the best position for you to be in.

💜 Live by faith.

❧ Application ❦

Try not to fight the transformation process which is taking place within you. Rest in the Lord's plan for the type of marriage He intended!

Rest in the LORD, and wait patiently for Him. Psalm 37:7

Lesson 25

The Bride of Christ

During the time I was seeking the Lord and asking Him what wives He wanted me to write about for this book, He took my breath away when He told me to write on this last wife. Reason being is that it is so fitting to close up the book with this wife. As the Lord closes up the bible with the book of Revelation, I'm closing up the *Wives of the Bible* with the Bride of Christ- the Church, seven churches to be more exact, found in the book of Revelation.

There's a beauty in the correlation between Jesus, the Bridegroom and His bride, the Church and our own marriages. It fascinates me how my marriage should be a reflection of the two. So when I started writing on the Bride of Christ I soon became saddened, convicted and inspired by the choices these Brides made.

At first mention of the book of Revelation, please don't freak out and be intimidated by it. I'm only going to share with you what God has to say about His bride.

In a nutshell, John writes letters to the seven churches and within those letters God gives each church a commendation or a complaint. As the letters are given to each church, I can't help but be challenged by my own actions and how I have been living my life when I read about these brides. When my life is over, I want to be known as the bride who was faithful to my Savior.

The Loveless Bride

To the Church of Ephesus...
> "I know all the things you do. I have seen your hard work and your patient endurance. I know you don't tolerate evil people. You have examined the claims of those who say they are apostles but are not. You have discovered they are liars. You have patiently suffered for me without quitting. "But I have this complaint against you. You don't love me or each other as you did at first! Rev. 2:2-4

At first reading, this bride starts our great. She's hardworking and patient, and she reminds me of a dutiful wife. But things take a turn for the worst when God says, "You don't love me or each other as you did at first!"

As wives, we can know the Word, be diligent, not tolerant of evil and suffer long for the Lord, but we should never lose our love for the Lord and for one another, more specifically, our husband.

The Persecuted Bride

To the Church of Smyrna…
> "I know about your suffering and your poverty—but you are rich! I know the blasphemy of those opposing you. They say they are Jews, but they are not, because their synagogue belongs to Satan. Rev. 2:9

This bride wasn't wealthy by material standards and she suffered and was persecuted for the Lord. I am fully acquainted with the emotions of this Bride and perhaps you are too? But in spite of the trials she endured, God commended her.

The Compromising Bride

To the Church of Pergamos…
> "I know that you live in the city where Satan has his throne, yet you have remained loyal to me. You refused to deny me even when Antipas, my faithful witness, was martyred among you there in Satan's city. "But I have a few complaints against you.

You tolerate some among you whose teaching is like that of Balaam, who showed Balak how to trip up the people of Israel. He taught them to sin by eating food offered to idols and by committing sexual sin. Rev. 2:13,14 (NLT)

This bride was faithful to Christ even when she was being martyred, but she was known as a compromising bride. She tolerated immorality, idolatry and false doctrine. These tolerances are so common in our world today but they grieve the Lord.

The Corrupt Bride

To the Church of Thyatira…
"I know all the things you do. I have seen your love, your faith, your service, and your patient endurance. And I can see your constant improvement in all these things. "But I have this complaint against you. You are permitting that woman—that Jezebel who calls herself a prophet—to lead my servants astray. She teaches them to commit sexual sin and to eat food offered to idols. Rev. 2:19-20 (NLT)

This bride was loving, faithful, patient, and a servant but she tolerated evil.

The Dead Bride

To the Church of Sardis...
"I know all the things you do, and that you have a reputation for being alive—but you are dead. Wake up! Strengthen what little remains, for even what is left is almost dead. I find that your actions do not meet the requirements of my God. Rev. 3:1-2

This bride had a reputation of being faithful to Jesus, but in reality, she wasn't.

The Faithful Bride

To the Church of Philadelphia...
"I know all the things you do, and I have opened a door for you that no one can close. You have little strength, yet you obeyed my word and did not deny me. Look, I will force those who belong to Satan's synagogue—those liars who say they are Jews but are not—to come and bow down at your feet. They will acknowledge that you are the ones I love. Rev. 3:8-9 (NLT)

She was a faithful bride even in the midst of little strength. She obeyed her Lord and did not deny Him.

The Lukewarm Bride

To the Church of Laodicea...
> "I know all the things you do, that you are neither hot nor cold. I wish that you were one or the other! But since you are like lukewarm water, neither hot nor cold, I will spit you out of my mouth! You say, 'I am rich. I have everything I want. I don't need a thing!' And you don't realize that you are wretched and miserable and poor and blind and naked. Rev. 3:15-17 (NLT)

Sadly, this bride was indifferent.

Lessons to Learn from the Bride of Christ...

- ♥ All seven of these brides knew the Lord.

- ♥ They all had a choice in how they were going to live their lives. Some were righteous and chose wisely, others were foolish, seeking to please themselves, or they sought to please man, instead of God.

Do not be deceived: God cannot be mocked. A man reaps what he sows. Whoever sows to please their flesh, from the flesh will reap destruction; whoever sows to please the Spirit, from the Spirit will reap eternal life. Gal. 6:7-8

❧ Application ❧

God has given each of one of us a choice on how we are going to live; we have been given free will. In the midst of the mundane and the suffering in our marital relationship, it's easy to lose sight of our permanent home in heaven when we get caught up in the trials and tribulations of our world, but my challenge to you is to keep your eyes fixed on the Lord.

Set your mind on things above, not on things on the earth.
Col. 3:2

Remain steadfast, lean on the Lord and rest in His promises. Be determined to pursue and strengthen your relationship with Jesus Christ and with your man.

And the God of all grace, who called you to his eternal
glory in Christ, after you have suffered a little while, will
himself restore you and make you strong, firm
and steadfast.
1 Peter 5:10

At the end of your life, which bride would you like to identify with?

Conclusion

Many times throughout the writing of this book I would mention to you about taking certain paths in your marriage while avoiding other ones. Reason being is because of what I've gleaned in the book of Proverbs. On numerous occasions Proverbs will mention the 'wise man' and the 'foolish man'. A simple definition of the two: a wise man is someone who fears the Lord and a foolish man is someone who doesn't fear the Lord. Because we are Godly wives, seeking to please our Savior, it's always best to take the wise path, but the wise path is not always the easiest one to take, sometimes it might require us to take copious amounts of dark chocolate and iced mochas with us while we walk (or crawl) this path!

In my life, I'm doing the best I can to walk *The Narrow Path* but I must tell you, I have grown weary, I've been wounded, I've wondered where my Savior was when I needed a reprieve from all my trials, and I've even wandered, but I've learned to keep on, keeping on. *The Narrow* Path is the *only* path that will lead to a flourishing marriage.

Your word is a lamp to my feet
and a light to my path. Psalm 119:105

Friend, it is my hope and prayer that you'll remain steadfast on *The Narrow Path* as well.

About the Author

Jolene Engle loves her God, her husband, her boys, and her small, white dog. She considers herself a reluctant, but obedient, author. She has dedicated her life to searching the Scriptures and applying God's truths to help Christian wives around the world experience a glorious marriage. She shows Christian women how to apply practical and biblical truths that encourage and inspire wives to live a life that is poured out for Christ like the perfume from an Alabaster Jar (Luke 7:37). You can find her sharing God's heart for equipping women at her on-line ministry site, The Alabaster Jar. Jolene and her family reside in Southern California.

To connect with Jolene:

Website- www.JoleneEngle.com
Facebook- https://www.facebook.com/JoleneNoelleEngle
Twitter- https://twitter.com/JoleneEngle
Pinterest- http://pinterest.com/joleneengle

Made in the USA
Lexington, KY
30 May 2014